A Civil War Christmas

AN AMERICAN MUSICAL CELEBRATION

A Civil War Christmas

AN AMERICAN MUSICAL CELEBRATION

Paula Vogel

Music by Daryl Waters

THEATRE COMMUNICATIONS GROUP
NEW YORK
2012

The photo on page xiii from the Long Wharf Theatre production was taken by T. Charles Erickson. From left to right: Ora Jones, Diane Sutherland, Brian Tyree Henry, Rachel Shapiro Alderman, J. D. Goldblatt, Guy Adkins and Drew McVety.

The publication of *A Civil War Christmas: An American Musical Celebration* through TCG's Book Program is made possible in part by the New York State Council on the Arts with the support of Governor Andrew Cuomo and the New York State Legislature.

CIP data information is on file at the Library of Congress, Washington, D.C.

ISBN: 978-1-55936-378-5

Book design and composition by Lisa Govan
Cover design by Lisa Govan
Cover art by Roland Sarkany

First Edition, March 2012

This play is dedicated to the children in my family:

Zachary, Nick, Greg, Kenny, Brian, Eric,
Carl Luke, Sam and Rebecca

AND

In memory of my mother-in-law:
Dorothy Sterling

Contents

Preface and Acknowledgments

*D*uring a dinner break while in tech at Berkeley Rep in 1997, I had dinner with my director Molly Smith. Molly had just gotten the job as artistic director at Arena Stage, and I broke forth: "Why are we doing *A Christmas Carol* about Victorian London poverty? Where is the American *Carol*?!" The play came to me in a flash: and with crayon on the paper table cloth, I diagrammed the play.

All of it spilled out—the battlefields around Washington, D.C. that I visited as a schoolgirl, the trips to the Peterson House opposite Ford's Theatre (where they brought the dying President Lincoln), the lyrics to our state song "Maryland, My Maryland" and all of the Civil War battle songs we learned in childhood . . . even the feeble efforts I made as a teenager, visiting Vietnam War soldiers at Walter Reed and Bethesda Naval hospitals, trying to solace working-class teenagers, only a few years older than I, who had been drafted into a war not of their own choosing.

Although I decided to develop this play at the home Long Wharf provided, my thanks to Molly Smith for that first discussion.

But the play might have remained words on paper passed from reader to reader had it not been for Chase Mishkin, whose support made it possible to explore this play from workshop to stage, and who helped give me one of the great productions of my life at Long Wharf. Thank you.

To Tina Landau, for the workshops and the premiere: I am still overwhelmed by your production.

My thanks to Daryl Waters: his amazing score, his unflappable presence, his soulful ear, his brilliance.

And as well to Andrew Resnick, our musical director, for launching the show each night in New Haven and Boston, and keeping musical vigil.

To Gordon Edelstein, and the entire company at Long Wharf: my thanks, my love. I have been so happy in your halls and rooms. It is wonderful at last to have a home in one of my hometowns.

I am honored by all of the companies and casts, the directors and designers, who have brought this show to fruition: Long Wharf, Huntington, TheatreWorks, Northlight, and the little company that could: New Haven Theater Company—a small community theater that produced the show with local actors.

And my gratitude as well:

To Jerry Patch, whose generous mind gave insightful notes, and whose company gave us courage;

To Jessica Thebus, who tackled this work in three weeks with unflagging spirit and gave us a gorgeous Christmas.

To Dan Ostling, whose visions haunt me still.

To Peter DuBois, to all the staff and folks at Huntington— I am grateful. To Robert Kelley, to BJ Jones, my thanks for the honor of being produced in your theaters.

My gratitude for the research by Michelle Hall, April Donahower, Charles Haugland, Katie McGerr, Krista Williams, Matt Cornish, Noëlle G-M Gibbs and all the dramaturgs.

I have been fortunate in my ensembles, the lovely actors, choruses, the children who tread the stage each night as troupers; so fortunate in the companies I keep.

Thanks to Kathy Smith, Washington, D.C. historian, for her insight and time. And to Carroll Gibbs, for his work and his encouragement. Many thanks to Jean Baker, for her work on Mary Todd Lincoln; to the remarkable historian Doris Kearns Goodwin and her book that I could re-read for another decade. And thanks to Anna Deveare Smith for her challenging mind and her encouragement. Thanks to Dr. Evelynn Hammonds for a great reading list.

Mark Brokaw did the impossible (yet again): directing a staged reading with a chorus in Independence, Kansas, in four days (perhaps I should not write this, in case artistic directors realize it can be done in four days). It is always a great honor to work with Mark, and I thank him.

And, oh, the chorus of citizens and students at the Inge Festival who had memorized the music and sounded heavenly— my gratitude.

I have trampled over Virginia ground with a lovely Mosby expert/impersonator; tussled over the war ("of Northern Aggression"!) with a Confederate reenactor at Washington and Lee University; argued with a John Brown impersonator who showed up in New Haven, perfectly attired, over the legitimacy of making up dialogue; and been corrected, gently and not so gently, over my historical mistakes by so many audience members. I am grateful to the folks from the National Trust for Historic Preservation who allowed me to walk through the Lincolns' summer cottage before it had been restored.

In the writing, dreaming, reading, and listening, it has taken a decade to make this play. It has taken more than a village—it has taken an army. My thanks to everyone who has helped me.

But beyond thanks, I am indebted to my wife, Anne, who listened to countless Christmas carols, spirituals and Civil War ballads, and who listened for well over a decade to the twists and turns of the plots. My thanks to friends and family for their support, love and forbearance.

I will always remember my mother-in law, Dorothy Sterling, every time I visit this playworld (she died two days before the Long Wharf opening). She was in her nineties as I researched and wrote this play, helped on by her thoughts, questions and generous use of her library. I am indebted to her conversation and her moral compass in the world. As the author of *Freedom Train, Lucretia Mott, Captain of the Planter, We Are Your Sisters* and *Mary Jane*, she had spent a lifetime making sure that children would know of this critical time in our country, and she witnessed and participated in our more recent struggles for civil rights and justice.

Her memory failing, she would ask that I read her the draft of this play over and over: a perfect audience of one, who had forgotten every plot point and was constantly surprised. She did, however, keenly remember the New Year's Eve Celebration of Emancipation in 1863 as if it were yesterday.

The making of theater shares much with the celebration of Christmas: there is the encroaching deadline. (How many shopping days left? How many previews before opening?) There is gift-wrapping and note writing and anticipation.

And there is melancholy mixed with the joy. Friendships lost, members of the family missing around the tree; the knowledge that the present company will disperse.

The first production was such a blessing, such a singular experience during the campaign of Barack Obama, that it makes me hopeful that companies in the future will experience such collaboration while working on this play. We kept saying, as the days of the run pushed us nearer to the close of the show: "Next year at Long Wharf!" We were of one mind—all of us vowed to work on the show together again.

Alas, that was not to be. In our company there was a wonderful actor, and a great soul: Guy Adkins. Guy was marvelous, essential theatrical glue to this production: popping up as John Wilkes Booth, as Robert E. Lee, here a union officer, there a mule. Sadly, shortly after our show closed, it was discovered that he was terminally ill. Anyone who has had the great good fortune to work with him can attest to what a loss the American theater has suffered.

But I am so thankful to have experienced his spirit onstage, his joy in the room, and his generous embrace of this play.

Paula Vogel
Providence, Rhode Island
2012

A Civil War Christmas

AN AMERICAN MUSICAL CELEBRATION

Production History

A Civil War Christmas: An American Musical Celebration received its world premiere at Long Wharf Theatre (Gordon Edelstein, Artistic Director; Joan Channick, Managing Director) in New Haven, Connecticut, on December 3, 2008. It was directed by Tina Landau; set design was by James Schuette, costume design was by Toni-Leslie James, lighting design was by Scott Zielinski, sound design was by Josh Horvath, the music was supervised, arranged and orchestrated by Daryl Waters; the music director was Andrew Resnick, the dramaturg was April Donahower and the production stage manager was Lori Lundquist. The cast was as follows:

HANNAH, ROSE, AGGY AND OTHERS	Bianca LaVerne Jones
CHESTER MANTON SAUNDERS, HAY, JOHN SURRATT AND OTHERS	Justin Blanchard
WILLY MACK, WALKER LEWIS, JIM WORMLEY AND OTHERS	Brian Tyree Henry
DECATUR BRONSON, JAMES WORMLEY AND OTHERS	Marc Damon Johnson
ABRAHAM LINCOLN, WALT WHITMAN AND OTHERS	Jay Russell
SILVER, ELY PARKER, FREDERICK WORMLEY, MOSES LEVY AND OTHERS	J. D. Goldblatt
JOHN WILKES BOOTH, ROBERT E. LEE, WILLIAM TECUMSEH SHERMAN AND OTHERS	Guy Adkins

MARY SURRATT, NICOLAY,	
CLARA BARTON,	
WIDOW SAUNDERS AND OTHERS	Rachel Shapiro Alderman
MARY TODD LINCOLN,	
SECRETARY OF WAR STANTON	
AND OTHERS	Diane Sutherland
MRS. ELIZABETH KECKLEY,	
MRS. ELIZABETH THOMAS AND OTHERS	Ora Jones
HENRY WADSWORTH LONGFELLOW,	
ULYSSES S. GRANT, WARD HILL LAMON,	
MOSBY RAIDER AND OTHERS	Drew McVety
LEWIS PAYNE, MOSBY RAIDER	
AND OTHERS	Scott Thomas
LITTLE JOE, JESSA	Faith Philpot, Malanky Wells
RAZ, ANNA SURRATT AND OTHERS	Susannah Flood

A Civil War Christmas. An American Musical Celebration was presented at Huntington Theatre Company (Peter DuBois, Artistic Director; Michael Maso, Managing Director) in Boston, Massachusetts, on November 18, 2009. It was directed by Jessica Thebus; set design was by Dan Ostling, costume design was by Miranda Hoffman, lighting design was by T. J. Gerckens, sound design was by Ben Emerson, the music was supervised, arranged and orchestrated by Daryl Waters; the musicians were Andrew Resnick (conductor/piano) and Morgan Evans-Weiler (fiddle), and the production stage manager was Gail P. Luna. The cast was as follows:

HANNAH, ROSE, AGGY, MATRON	Uzo Aduba
CHESTER MANTON SAUNDERS, HAY,	
JOHN SURRATT, UNION SOLDIER	Chris Bannow
WILLY MACK, WALKER LEWIS, JIM WORMLEY	Jason Bowen
DECATUR BRONSON, JAMES WORMLEY,	
PHILIP REID	Gilbert Glenn Brown

ABRAHAM LINCOLN, WALT WHITMAN,
SILVER   Ken Cheeseman
JOHN WILKES BOOTH, ROBERT E. LEE,
WILLIAM TECUMSEH SHERMAN,
MOSBY RAIDER 2, MARY SURRATT,
UNION SOLDIER   Ed Hoopman
MARY TODD LINCOLN, SECRETARY OF
WAR STANTON, WIDOW SAUNDERS   Karen MacDonald
ELY PARKER, GEORGE KECKLEY'S GHOST,
FREDERICK WORMLEY, MOSES LEVY,
LOUIS J. WEICHMANN,
REVEREND BROWN   DeLance Minefee
MRS. ELIZABETH KECKLEY,
MRS. ELIZABETH THOMAS   Jacqui Parker
HENRY WADSWORTH LONGFELLOW,
ULYSSES S. GRANT, WARD HILL LAMON,
LEWIS PAYNE, MOSBY RAIDER 1,
BURWELL, MINISTER   Stephen Russell
RAZ, ANNA SURRATT, NICOLAY,
CLARA BARTON, MULE   Molly Schreiber
JESSA   Alanna T. Logan,
                                             Hyacinth Tauriac

CHARACTERS

CHORUS

HANNAH

ROSE

AGGY

MATRON

CHESTER MANTON SAUNDERS

JOHN HAY

JOHN SURRATT

WILLY MACK LEE

WALKER LEWIS

JIM WORMLEY

DECATUR BRONSON

JAMES WORMLEY

PHILIP REID

ABRAHAM LINCOLN

WALT WHITMAN

SILVER

JOHN WILKES BOOTH

ROBERT E. LEE

WILLIAM TECUMSEH SHERMAN

MOSBY RAIDERS

MARY SURRATT

UNION SOLDIERS

MARY TODD LINCOLN

SECRETARY OF WAR STANTON

WIDOW SAUNDERS

ELY PARKER

GEORGE/GHOST OF GEORGE KECKLEY

FREDERICK WORMLEY

MOSES LEVY

LOUIS J. WEICHMANN

REVEREND ALEXANDER

MRS. ELIZABETH KECKLEY

MRS. ELIZABETH THOMAS

HENRY WADSWORTH LONGFELLOW

ULYSSES S. GRANT

WARD HILL LAMON

LEWIS PAYNE

MR. BURWELL

LITTLE JOE

MINISTER BINGHAM

RAZ

ANNA SURRATT

JOHN NICOLAY

CLARA BARTON

MULE

JESSA

MRS. JOHNSON

MATRON, ARMORY HOSTPITAL

SERGEANT-AT-ARMS

CORPORAL WILLS

SOLDIERS, WARD A

WHITE HOUSE SOLDIERS

BLACK UNION SOLDIERS

SOLDIERS, POINT LOOKOUT

LIEUTENANT AT EDWARD'S FERRY

LIEUTENANTS, 2ND RHODE ISLAND

MERCHANT

SENTRY

VENDOR
PENDEL
GUARD

PLACE

Washington, D.C., and along the Potomac River.

TIME

Christmastime, near the end of the Civil War.

Author's Notes

Music

All music in the play is public domain: Christmas carols, spirituals and Civil War ballads. It can and should be performed simply, with guitar, banjo, fiddle, percussion, piano—whatever is at hand. We've performed the score with a single musician/synthesizer and whatever the cast can add. I am fortunate in having Daryl Waters's score to guide us. (As a schoolgirl in Maryland, I was taught the lyrics to our state anthem, "Maryland, My Maryland" sung to the tune of "O Tannenbaum." It would take me a decade to realize that I had been taught the lyrics of a secessionist slave state song. When will the State of Maryland change the lyrics to that anthem?)

And if the audience sings along on some of the carols, better still.

Casting

This is the real fun of *A Civil War Christmas*, I think: the doubling, tripling and quadrupling of parts. The Chorus functions as does the Chorus in the adaptation of *Nicholas Nickleby*, that is, there's no static casting—one moment an actor plays a president, the next moment, he may play an assassin. It's up to each director and cast to play with the distribution of voices: African Americans may comment on the white Washingtonians, women may comment on men, and then there's the horse and the mule . . . and gender changes with a hat or a shawl.

The character of Raz is a nineteenth-century breeches role; the actress should be able to change her gender with a skirt, a cloak and a bonnet. Actors and directors should choose different voices and dialects for each role. (This helps keep the costume budget down!)

Setting/Costumes

It would be great if the cast pretty much stays on the stage, and we see their costume changes. The simpler, the better. This play has to move quickly; there's a lot of ground to cover.

It is possible to do this play with eight to twelve actors, and more than possible to do it with fourteen. But most of all, this is a play for community: so in some towns, perhaps it would be ideal to co-produce the play with local universities, undergraduates, acting students, church choirs, schoolchildren and, if there are any, Civil War reenactors.

SONGS

Act One

All Quiet/Silent Night	*Company*
I Heard the Bells	*Henry Wadsworth Longfellow,*
	Robert E. Lee, Ulysses S. Grant,
	Ely Parker, Abraham Lincoln
Take No Prisoners	
(Pounding Out His Vow)	*Decatur Bronson*
Follow the Drinking Gourd	*Company*
Gone Away to Shiloh	*Raz*
Jubilee	*William Tecumseh Sherman*
God Rest Ye	
Merry Gentlemen	*Company*
What Child Is This?	*Mrs. Elizabeth Keckley and Company*
Maryland, My Maryland	*John Wilkes Booth, Lewis Payne,*
	John Surratt
The Holly and the Ivy	*Ward Hill Lamon, Abraham Lincoln*
O Tannenbaum	*Ward Hill Lamon, Chorus 1–3*

Act Two

God Rest Ye Merry Gentlemen	*Mary Todd Lincoln*
Roll on Liberty Ball	*Widow Saunders*
Temple of Freedom	*Widow Saunders, Chester Manton Saunders*
Yellow Rose of Texas	*Decatur Bronson, Chorus of Soldiers*
There Is a Balm in Gilead	*Mrs. Elizabeth Keckley, Hannah*
Silent Night/Kaddish	*Mary Todd Lincoln, Moses Levy, Chorus 1–3*
Children, Go Where I Send Thee	*Black Chorus*
Ain't That A'Rocking	*Mrs. Elizabeth Keckley*
O Christmas Tree	*Company*
I Heard the Bells	*Company*

Act One

Scene 1

INTRODUCTION. WASHINGTON, D.C., CHRISTMAS EVE, 1864

Henry Wadsworth Longfellow/Chorus and Company

Bugles and drums fade into a winter wind as the Company comes on singing.

MEN:

    All quiet along
    The Potomac tonight
    Where the soldiers
    Lie peacefully
    Dreaming

WOMEN:

    Silent night,
    Holy night
    All is calm, all is bright

(Women hum.)

MEN:

    And their tents in the rays of the clear winter moon
    And the light of the campfires are gleaming

13

ALL:

> There's only the sound of the lone sentry's tread

MEN:

> As he tramps from the rock to the fountain.

(Women hum.)

CHORUS 1: Welcome to our story. The season is upon us, and whether it's Christmas, Hanukkah, Kwanzaa or New Year's—it's a time when we feel our connection to a larger community.

CHORUS 2: Our story takes place in the bustling city of Washington, D.C., and along the Potomac River. The Potomac has as many twists and turns as our story tonight: but here's all you need to know. On the northern side of the river— Edward's Ferry, the District of Columbia and Point Lookout. On the southern side, anywhere you can row—a presidential assassin might find safe harbor.

CHORUS 3: Most winters, December is gentle on the land that borders the Potomac: you can smell the promise of tilled earth and the harvest to come.

CHORUS 4 *(Singing)*:

> Sleep in heavenly peace

CHORUS 5: But not that blustery December of 1864. Four years of the most brutal harvesting of men have raged across both banks of this river.

CHORUS 4 *(Singing)*:

> Sleep in heavenly peace.

CHORUS 5: As if in wrath, the heavens have blasted the swift Potomac with ice from Edward's Ferry all the way to Wash– ington, so thick with ice you could almost step across.

14

CHORUS 6: On the northern side of the Potomac, nurses at the Armory Hospital pile blankets on the rows of Union soldiers in their beds.

(The wind howls.)

It's going to be a cold one tonight.

CHORUS 7: Five hundred miles to the north of Armory Hospital, the same blustery wind rattles a poet's windows in Massa—chusetts. Henry Wadsworth Longfellow paces in his Cam—bridge study; all day he'd had some strange feeling in his bones as he listened to the wind. And so Longfellow put another log on his fire, sat at his desk, put pen in hand and wrote:

LONGFELLOW/CHORUS *(Spoken)*:

> I heard the bells on Christmas Day
> Their old, familiar carols play
> And wild and sweet
> The words repeat
> Of peace on earth, goodwill to men!

(Singing:)

> I thought how, as the day had come
> The belfries of all Christendom
> Had rolled along
> The unbroken song
> Of peace on earth, goodwill to men!

Scene 2

ON THE SOUTH SIDE OF THE POTOMAC: COFFEE

Willy Mack/Chorus and Robert E. Lee

WILLY MACK/CHORUS: And across the banks of the Potomac, three wise men sit and stare into their fires. Our first wise man stares into the very future itself. And just as he has for the past thirty years of his life, Willy Mack serves his Master, General Robert E. Lee.

(Willy Mack presents a mug.)

LEE: What is that?

WILLY MACK: Liquid gold, Marse Bob: one hundred percent Yankee coffee.

LEE: No thank you. I still have the taste of that pisswater you brewed me last time—brewed twigs, bark—how did you get the water to turn brown? Second thought—do not tell me.

WILLY MACK: I gave you what the men are drinking during the siege. But now—smell it.

LEE *(Breathes it in)*: O Lord—it's actually coffee.

WILLY MACK: A gift from Colonel Mosby. One of his Raiders made it through the lines. Merry Christmas.

LEE *(Inhales one more time)*: No. Thank you. If my men can't have coffee, I can't have coffee. Please present it to the officers with my compliments.

WILLY MACK: Yes, sir.

(Pause. We hear a halfhearted refrain by the men of "O Come All Ye Faithful," which then dies out.)

Your men are too cold to sleep . . . Sir? You should turn in.

LEE: If my men can't sleep, I can't sleep. *(Beat)* We've lost.

WILLY MACK: Yes sir . . . you have.

(Lee looks at Willy Mack.)

We have.

LEE: I would gladly spill every drop of my blood if it would save my country.

WILLY MACK: It'd be a waste of blood now, Marse Bob . . . Sir? I should deliver this coffee before it turns cold . . .

LEE: Yes, yes, go on . . .

(Willy Mack withdraws, lifts the mug in a toast.)

WILLY MACK/CHORUS: To the officers! *(He drains the cup: "Ahhhh."*
   To us) Lee would stay up with his men tonight until dawn.
   How he longed to hear the bells of Christ Church in
   Alexandria once again! For the bells in every church in the
   South had fallen silent, melted into cannonballs.

LEE *(Singing)*:
>   Then from each gun's accursed mouth
>   The cannon thundered in the South
>   And with the sound
>   The carols drowned
>   Of peace on earth, goodwill to men.

Scene 3

COFFEE IN THE NORTHERN CAMP

*Ely Parker/Chorus, Ulysses S. Grant,
Secretary of War Stanton/Chorus and Company*

PARKER/CHORUS: And less than a mile away, enter Ely Parker,
   Seneca Indian, and aide-de-camp. Parker waited on his
   friend, a down-on-his-luck harness salesman whom Parker
   had befriended in Illinois a few years before.
CHORUS 2: You know what the moral of this story is? Be kind to
   clerks, secretaries and harness salesmen because you never
   know when they will end up to be—
PARKER: —General Grant, sir. Merry Christmas.
CHORUS 2: Parker had his secret orders from the Secretary of
   War Stanton himself:

STANTON/CHORUS: For the sake of the Union! Keep General
    Grant on the wagon for the duration of the war.
PARKER: Fresh-brewed coffee, sir.

(Parker presents the mug.)

GRANT: I'd rather drink my way into Christmas Oblivion.
PARKER: No sense in wasting good coffee . . .

(Grant reluctantly sips the coffee.)

GRANT: It's very good . . .

(Parker watches until Grant drains the cup.)

There! Satisfied?
PARKER: Is there anything else I may get for you?
GRANT: Oh, stop being my nursemaid and join me!

*(The two men warm themselves by the fire. Suddenly a boisterous
burst of music from Grant's men, erupting into laughter.)*

Our men are merry tonight . . . God forgive me, Parker.
I have walked across a bridge made from the bodies of my
fallen men, three men thick. But if I could, I would walk on
that bridge of bodies all the way to Richmond tonight, and
finish this bloody business off! But . . . it's Christmas Eve.

*(The two men relax; suddenly, in the silence, another clatter from
the mess tent.)*

Men in camp awaiting their Christmas dinner . . . it's music.
(Beat) I will never feel more peaceful than this night.
PARKER *(To us)*: For the hope of peace is sweeter than peace
    itself.

GRANT AND PARKER *(Singing)*:
> It was as if an earthquake rent
> The hearth-stones of a continent
> And made forlorn
> The households born
> Of peace on earth, goodwill to men!

Scene 4

"THREE WISE MEN . . . BOWED THEIR HEADS AND PRAYED."

Ulysses S. Grant, Robert E. Lee, Abraham Lincoln and Company

Music under as lights rise on Abraham Lincoln.

CHORUS 1: And Abraham Lincoln stared into his fire at the White House, less than fifteen miles away. He'd had that dream again last night—the dream he never told to his wife.
CHORUS 2: He found himself on the deck of some vast ship racing towards a distant shore.
CHORUS 1: That dream always gave him some strange feeling in his bones . . .

("I Heard the Bells" continues:)

LINCOLN *(Singing)*:
> And in despair I bowed my head
> "There is no peace on earth," I said;
> "For hate is strong
> And mocks the song
> Of peace on earth, goodwill to men!"

CHORUS 3: And in that moment, three wise men, on opposite shores of the Potomac, bowed their heads and prayed:

LEE, GRANT AND LINCOLN:
> Then pealed the bells more loud and deep;
> "God is not dead, nor doth he sleep;
> THE COMPANY
> The wrong shall fail
> The right prevail
> With peace on earth, goodwill to men!"

Scene 5

EDWARD'S FERRY SUPPLY DEPOT:
MEET DECATUR BRONSON, BLACKSMITH

Decatur Bronson, Rose, Lieutenant at Edward's Ferry and
Black Soldier 1 and 2/Chorus

BLACK SOLDIER 1 / CHORUS: And much farther up on the northern side of the Potomac, in a Union supply depot at Edward's Ferry:

BLACK SOLDIER 2 / CHORUS: Decatur Bronson blacksmiths for the army—

BRONSON *(Singing)*:
> Take no prisoners

(Bang! Bronson strikes the anvil.)

> Take no prisoners

(Bang!)

> Take no prisoners . . .

(Bang! A white Lieutenant pops his head into the smithy.)

LIEUTENANT: How's it coming, boy?

BRONSON: Fine, sir. If I can just work all night, I'll be done with your horses by Christmas.

LIEUTENANT: Or should I call you "Sergeant"? I hear you finished off a troop of Confederates single-handed. I hear you might get a Medal of Honor: that's some pretty killing of white men. So how would you like to be called?

BRONSON: You can call me what you like. Sir. Do you mind if I keep working? It's best if I put my hands to use . . .

LIEUTENANT: At ease. Carry on.

(The Lieutenant watches, still curious.)

So why on earth did you transfer? Staff Sergeant of Company A! You get tired of your men saluting you?

BRONSON: I was told I could get a pass. We own a farm around here. I'd like to see my folks.

LIEUTENANT: You own your own farm?

BRONSON: Yes, sir. I own myself, too . . . or I used to, before I joined the army. Sir? If I finish by morning—

LIEUTENANT: Yes, Bronson, you'll get your pass. I'll have Chester bring you your supper.

(The Lieutenant exits.)

BRONSON: Merry Christmas!

(Bronson's wife, Rose, appears in his imagination.)

ROSE: There are two R's in Marry. —There are two R's in Marry! —There are—

BRONSON *(Overlapping)*: Rose, I can't be thinking of you now. *(To drown her out:)*

Take no prisoners

21

(Bang!)

Take no prisoners.

(Bang! Bronson's Black Union soldiers appear behind him.)

Scene 6

TWO WEEKS AGO: POINT LOOKOUT AND THE VOW

Black Soldier 1 and 2 and Decatur Bronson

BLACK SOLDIER 1: Two weeks ago, Sergeant Decatur Bronson was in charge of his company on guard duty at Point Lookout.

BLACK SOLDIER 2: Point Lookout is a low strip of land where the Potomac empties into the sea. Here thousands of Confederate prisoners shiver in the blockade, guarded by—us: Company A, United States Colored Infantry.

BLACK SOLDIER 1: Some of our men recognize their former slave owners in the prison camp . . . and we get to give them orders at the point of our guns. Someone in the War Department has a sense of humor.

(The Black Soldiers watch Bronson march back and forth; Bronson whispers feverishly:)

BRONSON: Where is she? Where is she?

BLACK SOLDIER 2: He does this every day? In this weather?!

BLACK SOLDIER 1: He's losing his mind over his wife Rose.

BLACK SOLDIER 2: What happened to his—?

BLACK SOLDIER 1: The only time he stops thinking of her is when he works. When he fights. When he kills.

BLACK SOLDIER 2: Here— *(Black Soldier 2 gives a paper to Black Soldier 1)* You've fought with him. You present him with the orders for today.

BLACK SOLDIER 1: All right. Stand beside me.

BRONSON: (Where is she? Where is she?)

(The Black Soldiers present themselves to Bronson. They stand at attention and salute.)

BLACK SOLDIER 1: Sergeant Decatur Bronson! Requesting permission to present and execute orders for the day!

BRONSON: At ease, men. *(Bronson reads the paper)* What kind of fool order is this?! The order for today, December 14th: "No coffee will be given to the Confederate prisoners!"

BLACK SOLDIER 2: You can bet the rebs aren't giving any coffee to our prisoners.

BLACK SOLDIER 1: What do you mean, "our prisoners"? There aren't any colored prisoners.

BRONSON: You must be the new recruit.

BLACK SOLDIER 2: Yes, sir. Joined up last week.

BRONSON: Well, Private, here's something you need to know in battle. And never forget. This past spring, another regiment of our soldiers valiantly fought the Battle of Fort Pillow. They were surrounded by Confederates, and they surrendered. And those rebels rounded up the black Union troops who had thrown down their guns . . .

(Bronson kneels, and Black Soldier 1 follows; a beat late, Black Soldier 2 kneels.)

. . . and where our soldiers knelt in the fields . . .

(Bronson puts his hands behind his head; the others follow.)

BLACK SOLDIER 1: . . . Hands behind their heads . . .

BRONSON: The Confederates put a bullet through the brain of every last man.

(Echo of gunfire; Bronson helps Black Soldier 2 back to his feet.)

Every soldier in my command has a vow he yells before battle.

BRONSON AND BLACK SOLDIER 1: Take no prisoners!

BRONSON: It's a white man's privilege to starve to death in a prison camp.

BLACK SOLDIER 2: Sergeant? Should we execute the orders?

BRONSON: I'd rather execute the prisoners. *(Turns away)*

BLACK SOLDIER 2 *(To Black Soldier 1)*: What happened to his wife?

BLACK SOLDIER 1: The Texans on the run after Gettysburg stole her—a free-born woman—just took her off her own front porch. The sergeant joined up the next day.

BRONSON *(To himself)*: Every Confederate I kill is a bridge to reach her . . . but down here, the river is too wide . . . not even a regiment of bodies can reach across. *(Back to the Black Soldiers)* I've had it with this! I'm volunteering for a work transfer to the white supply depot at Edward's Ferry. *(To himself)* The river up there is barely a creek, two or three bodies wide. I'll feel closer to Rose up there near our farm. *(Back to the men)* Look for me in the spring when they move us to the field. We'll revenge Fort Pillow.

BLACK SOLDIER 1: When we take to the field to fight . . .

BLACK SOLDIER 2: If we get the chance in battle . . .

BRONSON: Away from our captain's eyes . . .

(The three men join hands to vow.)

BRONSON AND BLACK SOLDIER 1 AND 2: Take no prisoners!

(Bronson moves back to his anvil, back to work.)

Scene 7

EDWARD'S FERRY, CHRISTMAS EVE: POUNDING OUT
HIS VOW / "FOLLOW THE DRINKING GOURD."

Decatur Bronson, Black Soldier 1 and 2/Chorus and Company

BLACK SOLDIER 2: And that is how our Sergeant Bronson ended
up blacksmithing on Christmas Eve: pounding out his vow
on an anvil of rage.

BLACK SOLDIER 1 AND 2 *(Singing)*:
Take no prisoners!

BRONSON *(In a whisper)*: Where is she?

BLACK SOLDIER 1 AND 2 *(Singing)*:
Take no prisoners!

BRONSON *(In a whisper)*: Where is she?

BLACK SOLDIER 1 AND 2 *(Singing)*:
Take no prisoners!

BRONSON *(In a whisper)*: Where is she? *(Looks at the sky)* There's
the first star of the evening . . . Rose, wherever you are, if you
can look for the Big Dipper, the Drinking Gourd, you can
find your way North and back to me. Look for the Drinking
Gourd, and— *(Singing:)*

Follow the drinking gourd!

BLACK SOLDIER 1 AND 2/CHORUS:
Follow the drinking gourd!

BRONSON:

> For the old man is waiting to carry you to freedom

BLACK SOLDIER 1 AND 2/CHORUS:

> If you follow the drinking gourd
> The riverbank makes a mighty good road

BRONSON AND BLACK SOLDIER 1 AND 2/CHORUS:

> Dead trees will show you the way.
> Left foot, peg foot, traveling on;

BLACK SOLDIER 1 AND 2/CHORUS:

> Follow the drinking gourd!

ALL:	BRONSON:
Follow the drinking gourd!	We've got to follow . . .
Follow the drinking gourd!	Follow . . .

ALL:

> For the old man is waiting for to carry you to freedom.

Scene 8

BEWARE OF SLAVE CATCHERS;
FIFTEEN MILES SOUTH OF THE POTOMAC

Hannah, Jessa, Black Chorus and Company

"Follow the Drinking Gourd" continues:

HANNAH *(Singing)*:

> If you follow the drinking gourd . . .

CHORUS 1: On the southern side of the Potomac, Hannah and
   her daughter Jessa march North toward freedom:
JESSA: How much farther?

HANNAH: Just a couple more bends in the road. We got one more big river to cross.

JESSA: I want to go home.

HANNAH: It's not "home" since they sold your father. It's not "home" if you and I can't learn to read. It's not "home" if we can't go up the road without a paper we couldn't be taught to read saying we got permission to go up the road! So! We're gonna find us a "home" where I don't have to watch your back when you get older. Or worry about the Master selling you. Mr. Lincoln said we're free, and God gave us legs to walk.

JESSA *(Unmoved)*: I'm hungry.

HANNAH *(Undeterred by Jessa's lack of enthusiasm)*: When we cross the next big river, we're going to be in the United States of America. And the president there, it's his job to feed people who don't have any food, and to find a roof for people who don't have any houses. So let's get moving! But you listen up: if we get parted on this side or the other, you've got to be careful. Watch out for slave catchers.

JESSA: What do they look like?

HANNAH: If some white man comes up to you and acts nice, and asks where you live, who your mama is, are you lost—you get away from him! Don't answer. No slave catcher's going to get you.

(Jessa looks scared.)

Look, baby, the stars are coming out. See? There's the North Star. If you can read the stars, you can find your way North. *(Singing:)*

Follow the drinking gourd . . .

We're going to follow the stars just like the Three Wise Men did. *(Singing:)*

There's a star in the east on Christmas morn

BLACK CHORUS:

Rise up, Shepherd, and follow

HANNAH:

It will lead to the place where the Savior's born

BLACK CHORUS:

Rise up, Shepherd, and follow

WOMEN:

Follow, follow

ALL:

Rise up, Shepherd, and follow

WOMEN:

Follow the star to Bethlehem

ALL:

Rise up, Shepherd, and follow

WOMEN:

Leave your sheep and leave your lambs

ALL:

Rise up, Shepherd, and follow

WOMEN:

Leave your ewes and leave your rams

ALL:

Rise up, Shepherd, and follow . . .
Rise up, Shepherd, and follow . . .

(Hannah and Jessa hurry offstage.)

Scene 9

A FARM

Raz, Silver and Company

Raz and Silver begin to tiptoe out of the tool shed.

CHORUS 1: And a few miles away, a thirteen-year-old Virginian boy was staring up at the same evening star through the charred rafters of the tool shed. *(Snoring is heard)* The tool shed was all that was left after Union soldiers had torched all the farms, the crops, the fields in the valley. On one side of Raz Franklin lay his father, on his other side the only horse they could hide from the Yankees' raid. Raz decided tonight was the night to follow the stars to daring deeds! To revenge! To glory! And most of all, away from his father's snoring!

(Raz leads his horse, Silver—a member of the ensemble—quietly out of the shed. Silver is not dainty.)

RAZ: Silver, come on girl . . . Dang, Silver, shhh, quiet now girl . . .

CHORUS 2: He'd heard there was a company of Colonel Mosby's Raiders camping under the stars, close by the river. This was his chance to fight for the Confederacy! And so Raz tiptoed out of the tool shed like a teenager past curfew, stealing his favorite horse—

RAZ *(To us):* —I'm just borrowing her, really—

CHORUS 1: —Bound to join the feared Mosby Raiders! The darlings of the Confederacy, the curse of every Yankee!

RAZ *(Singing):*
> I put my knapsack on my back
> My rifle on my shoulder—

29

(Raz's Father snorts, starts, turns over and snores.)

CHORUS 1: If the fool didn't get caught first by his father and given a horsewhipping!

(Silver is alarmed; Raz croons to his horse softly:)

RAZ:

> I'm a-gone away to Shiloh
> And there I'll be a soldier . . .

(Silver nuzzles Raz, and Raz nuzzles right back.)

CHORUS 2: Oh, the love between a boy and his horse.
RAZ: Silver was the star of the stable.
CHORUS 2: She was meant to lead a cavalry charge against the Northern foe:
RAZ: Like Robert E. Lee's Traveller!

(Silver neighs in agreement.)

Like Stonewall Jackson's Little Sorrel!

(Another neigh.)

Like Highfly, Fire-eater, Nellie Gray! . . . Alas, some of these gallant horses paid the ultimate price of glory!

(Silver's head jerks up suddenly: "What?!")

But we'll ride together into immortality, my friend!

(Silver starts backing toward the farm; Raz is suddenly alone.)

Silver? Silver!?

(Raz catches Silver's reins.)

Come on, girl! Onward to Fame!

(Silver doesn't budge.)

To Fortune!

(Nothing doing.)

To Food!

(At that, Silver agrees to be led. The horse and Raz dance while Raz sings:)

> I put my knapsack on my back
> My rifle on my shoulder
> I'm a-gone away to Shiloh
> And there I'll be a soldier.

Scene 10

AT THE WHITE HOUSE

Walker Lewis/Chorus, Abraham Lincoln,
William Tecumseh Sherman/Chorus and Company

Sherman's reached Savannah.

WALKER/CHORUS: And if you follow the star due North, about fifteen miles or so, you'll come to a big White House on Pennsylvania Avenue, where Walker Lewis hurried through the corridors to President Lincoln. Walker's philosophy: "Hear No Evil, See No Evil"—but whisper all to my wife each night on our pillows—Mr. President.

(Lincoln is startled from his reverie. A clock chimes four o'clock.)

LINCOLN: Walker.

WALKER: Mr. Stanton just got this telegram over at War and asked
me to deliver it.

LINCOLN *(Expecting bad news)*: Let's have it then.

(A spotlight illuminates General William Tecumseh Sherman.)

SHERMAN/CHORUS: To His Excellency, President Lincoln: I beg
to present you, as a Christmas gift, the city of Savannah.
—William Tecumseh Sherman. *(Singing:)*

> Bring the good ol' bugle boys! We'll sing another song
> Sing it with a spirit that will start the world along
> Sing it like we used to sing it fifty thousand strong,
> While we were marching through Georgia.

ALL:

> Hurrah! Hurrah! We bring the jubilee
> Hurrah! Hurrah! The flag that makes you free
> So we sang the chorus from Atlanta to the sea
> While we were marching through Georgia—

LINCOLN: Sherman's reached Savannah! I've got to find the boys
and show them this!

Scene 11

WHITE HOUSE: "WHAT DO WE DO WITH DEATH THREATS?" /
MRS. LINCOLN'S GIFT

*John Nicolay/Chorus, John Hay, Abraham Lincoln
and Company*

NICOLAY/CHORUS: Right then Lincoln's secretaries,
HAY: Hay,

NICOLAY: and Nicolay, were sorting through the day's mail . . .

HAY: What do we do with death threats?

NICOLAY: Give 'em to Ward Hill Lamon.

HAY: He resigned yesterday. Said the president wasn't taking his personal safety seriously enough.

NICOLAY: The president refused his resignation—better take it to Mr. Lamon by hand.

(Just then Lincoln bursts in, waving the telegram. Hay hides the death threat behind his back. The boys gather around Lincoln and read the telegram.)

LINCOLN *(Singing)*:
> Hurrah! Hurrah! We bring the jubilee!
> Hurrah! Hurrah!—

LINCOLN, HAY AND NICOLAY:
> The flag that makes you free

ALL:
> So we sang the chorus from Atlanta to the sea
> While we were marching through Georgia!

NICOLAY: Congratulations, Mr. President!

HAY: I'll bet you Mrs. Lincoln will far prefer this stocking stuffing to the other gifts you've bought her.

LINCOLN: Oh Lord. What is tonight?

(Hay and Nicolay exchange looks.)

HAY: It's Christmas Eve, sir.

LINCOLN: Oh, no . . . I forgot . . . My wife . . .

NICOLAY: We can pop out and get something festive!

LINCOLN: No, no, no! I bought her something last summer . . . Ordered from Paris! Yes, sir, Mary thinks I don't pay attention, but I heard her talking with Mrs. Keckley, and bought her those imported kid gloves she prefers . . . only thing is, I hid them in the summer cottage, and just plumb forgot them there.

HAY: Perhaps you could give the First Lady an IOU in a nice gift-wrapped box?

LINCOLN: I'd rather face the Army of Northern Virginia with a pea shooter. I have to ride up to the summer cottage tonight and retrieve them.

HAY: Sir, that's an hour riding in the cold; if you just tell me where—

LINCOLN: A Christmas gift must come from my own hands to hers. I'll fetch it myself. Isn't there a gala you two must attend this evening at the War Department?

NICOLAY: Sir: it's not safe. Ward Hill Lamon has given us orders to—

LINCOLN: My God, can't a man have a moment alone in peace to breathe!

(Beat.)

It's safe if no one knows I'll be out riding tonight— *(He sees Hay is hiding something)* What do you have there, Hay?

HAY: Nothing, sir. Just a letter.

LINCOLN: I'll take care of it.

(Reluctantly Hay hands it over.)

"I have it on good authority, sirs, that there is a den of traitors meeting in Widow Mary Surratt's boarding house on H Street in this very city—" *(Lincoln crumples the letter and tosses it)* There. I took care of it. By Executive Order there will be no more work today, December 24, 1864—

(We hear a clock ping as he checks his watch.)

4:15 P.M.

NICOLAY: Thank you, Mr. President.

HAY: Will you please wish your family and Mrs. Lincoln Merry Christmas when next you see her?

LINCOLN: It will be quite some time before I see her next . . . She's shopping . . .

(Lincoln exits. Hay retrieves the death threat and uncrumples it.)

Scene 12

PENNSYLVANIA AVENUE: "OOOOH, WHAT LOVELY CLOTH!" / "A CHRISTMAS TREE?"

*Mary Todd Lincoln, Mrs. Elizabeth Keckley,
Merchant/Chorus and Company*

MERCHANT/CHORUS: And at that same hour Mary Todd Lincoln and Elizabeth Keckley walked arm-in-arm past the shops on Pennsylvania Avenue.

(A Merchant rushes forth with a bolt of expensive cloth.)

MARY TODD LINCOLN: Ooooh, what lovely cloth!

(Mrs. Keckley smiles a no, and the two continue:)

We have been reprieved by Mr. Lincoln's reelection. Oh, Lizzie, I will scrimp until all the bills are paid . . . if he had lost, we would have gone from the White House to the poor house!

(They pass another shop; a Woman rushes out with hats in hand. Mrs. Lincoln stops.)

Ohh! The feather is adorable!

(Mrs. Keckley with a critical eye passes on the hats.)

If Mr. Lincoln found out how much I have charged on credit! . . . Oh, Lizzie, the storm! I will never buy another item of clothing or jewelry for . . . well, the next year, at least.

KECKLEY: Mrs. Lincoln, I can fit all of your dresses with new lace and such flourishes, they will astonish your company still!

MARY TODD LINCOLN: I have seen the carriages of Washington matrons lined up at your door, ordering their gowns for the Inaugural Ball . . . and I will have to wear last year's fashion—your fashion, dear Lizzie, and the best to be had in 1863 . . . but I do have to present a certain appearance as the wife of the Head of State—and it's actually your reputation at stake as well. The ladies of this town are unforgiving.

KECKLEY: We will dazzle the ladies of the town; after my hands are put to use, no one will recognize your gown.

(The Shoemaker comes forth with slippers.)

MARY TODD LINCOLN: And such a storm of criticism for my refitting the White House! The carpets were stained from the spittoons, and people had cut up the curtains for souvenirs! What would our foreign dignitaries say back home? —Oh! Wouldn't these slippers be darling with my burgundy moiré?

KECKLEY: Mrs. Lincoln, remember, now, your vow!

(Mrs. Keckley moves Mrs. Lincoln away.)

MARY TODD LINCOLN: You have no idea how much we owe— Lizzie, I must tell someone, it has been such a burden—

KECKLEY: Do not tell me. It is better if someone asks me that I can say I do not know.

(The ladies walk on.)

Let's look for a few things for Tad . . . perhaps a drum to replace the one he broke? And I thought we'd agreed that you would make something with your hands, something homemade for the rest—

MARY TODD LINCOLN: My hands are useless.

KECKLEY: There is a merchant with toys up ahead, and his prices are reasonable . . .

(They stop in front of a Merchant displaying a small Union uniform for a little boy.)

MARY TODD LINCOLN: Oh—oh, look, Lizzie—a little uniform just like the one Willie used to wear!

(Mrs. Keckley finds a handkerchief as Mrs. Lincoln weeps, and motions the Merchant to withdraw.)

MERCHANT/CHORUS: Willie, her third son, his father's joy, had died of typhoid fever almost two years ago, and Mary Todd Lincoln still wore mourning.

KECKLEY: Mrs. Lincoln, Mrs. Lincoln, there now, there now. It's Christmas Eve.

MARY TODD LINCOLN: Oh, Lizzie, how thoughtless of me. I still have Tad and Robert for my old age, and you have lost George, your only son!

(Mrs. Lincoln now weeps for Mrs. Keckley. From a distance, the Ghost of George Keckley appears on the street. Mrs. Keckley turns away and touches the cloth of the uniform held by the Merchant, controlling herself.)

CHORUS 1: Mrs. Keckley had bought freedom for herself and her son only five years ago with money saved from her needle and thread. Then she stitched some more to send her son to college. But George, light-skinned enough to pass as a white man, ran away from school to join the Union. He died in the very first battle he fought.

(The Ghost of George Keckley retreats.)

KECKLEY: We've got to remember the living. To keep busy! I promised my ladies I'd finish up our orders by now.

MARY TODD LINCOLN *(A thought stops her weeping)*: —You don't think that perhaps one new outfit for me would please Mr. Lincoln tonight? Something to make me look softer, a bit younger, a bit more festive?

KECKLEY: That's impossible! *(Regaining her diplomacy)* —I mean, it's not possible for you to look prettier than you do right now. Forgive me, Mrs. Lincoln, after I finish up with my sewing, I promised to be at the Children's Home by nine . . . I have a special treat for them tonight—a Christmas tree!

MARY TODD LINCOLN: A Christmas tree?

Scene 13

TWO WEEKS AGO: MRS. KECKLEY VISITS THE WORMLEYS' SHOP

Mrs. Elizabeth Keckley/Chorus, James Wormley/Chorus and Frederick and Jim Wormley

KECKLEY/CHORUS: Two weeks ago, I paid a visit to the one person in Washington who can find anything for anybody—

JAMES WORMLEY/CHORUS: Shopkeeper, hack carriage company owner and all-around entrepreneur.

KECKLEY/CHORUS: My friend, a Mr. James Wormley . . .

(James Wormley and his two sons wait on Mrs. Keckley in his shop.)

JAMES WORMLEY: —A tree! Now that is a problem. Every tree has been cut for the soldiers' campfires for miles around and pine . . . we'll have to go north of the city. Pine makes a terrible fire.

KECKLEY: I want to make a Christmas tree for the children in the home.

JAMES WORMLEY: Oh yes, I've heard of that. Isn't that a Bavarian custom? We usually just deck the halls with boughs of holly— *(Calling out)* Frederick? Jim? Can you boys get a cart next week up to the country and cut a pine tree?

FREDERICK: Yes, sir!

JIM: Anything for you, Mrs. Keckley.

KECKLEY: I knew I could rely on you! Just name your price, Mr. Wormley.

JAMES WORMLEY: It will be our pleasure to contribute it to the home.

KECKLEY: Gracious thanks! I'll be by on Christmas Eve. Good day, gentlemen . . .

(The three Wormleys jump to get the door. Simultaneously:)

FREDERICK AND JIM: JAMES WORMLEY:
—I'll get the door! . . .   —Allow me!

(James Wormley escorts Mrs. Keckley out, then returns. The men sigh.)

FREDERICK: Mrs. Keckley is easy on the eyes, don't you think, Papa?

JAMES WORMLEY *(Slapping Frederick upside his head)*: I may be married to your mother, but I'm not dead.

Scene 14

BACK TO THE PRESENT: SHOPPING / MRS. KECKLEY
HAD A STRANGE FEELING IN HER BONES

Mrs. Elizabeth Keckley, Mary Todd Lincoln, Jessa and Hannah

The present: Mrs. Keckley strolls down the street with Mrs. Lincoln.

MARY TODD LINCOLN: A Christmas tree?

KECKLEY: Yes! A Christmas tree.

MARY TODD LINCOLN: But who these days keeps a Christmas tree? Isn't that a foreign custom? Isn't that a bit, well, pagan?

(Bells chime the hour: five o'clock.)

KECKLEY: I must go.

MARY TODD LINCOLN: You are so good for my spirits, Lizzie. The president and I have a small gift for the home. *(She hands Mrs. Keckley some money)* You are doing so much for those poor women and children!

KECKLEY: Thank you both so much, Mrs. Lincoln.

MARY TODD LINCOLN: But isn't there something we can get just for you?

KECKLEY: There is something I would very much like. I would like to have the glove that Mr. Lincoln wears to his second Inaugural Ball.

MARY TODD LINCOLN: His glove! After the Ball! Why on earth would you want a soiled and sweaty glove! I won't wear a pair of gloves twice!

KECKLEY: I want the glove from the hand that signed the Emancipation Proclamation.

MARY TODD LINCOLN: You are a strange woman!

KECKLEY: That is what I would like.

40

MARY TODD LINCOLN: All right, then. His glove!

(Lights up on Jessa, standing still, shivering in a blanket wrapped around her. Hannah rushes back, lifts her daughter, and hurries off, carrying Jessa in her arms. Mrs. Keckley shivers in the street.)

Are you all right?

KECKLEY: I've been cold all day. Some strange feeling in my bones.

MARY TODD LINCOLN: You're working too hard . . . Lizzie . . . my hands are useless! I must buy a gift for Mr. Lincoln. Do you have any ideas?

KECKLEY: May I speak as a friend of the family?

MARY TODD LINCOLN: Please . . .

KECKLEY: The president doesn't care for things. The best thing you can give your husband this Christmas would be . . . just give him the gladness of your heart. Would you do that?

MARY TODD LINCOLN: The gladness of my heart . . . yes, yes, I will do that. Merry Christmas, Mrs. Keckley!

(The two embrace; Mrs. Keckley dashes off.)

—I wonder where in all of Washington, D.C., one could buy a Christmas tree?

Scene 15

AT THE POTOMAC: "STEP BACK, WOMAN,
IF YOU DON'T HAVE A PASS."

Hannah, Jessa and Sentry/Chorus

Hannah, carrying a cold and exhausted Jessa, is stopped by a Union Sentry.

SENTRY: Halt.

HANNAH: Excuse me, sir . . . what's the name of this big river?

SENTRY: The Potomac. You've reached the Long Bridge.

HANNAH: And on the other side . . .

SENTRY: Washington, D.C.

(Just then a church tower chimes five o'clock.)

HANNAH: Jessa—there are bells here! *(To the Sentry)* We haven't heard bells in some time.

SENTRY: You have to step back, woman, if you don't have a pass.

HANNAH: Sir, just let me explain: we've been traveling four, five days, and we just need to get to Washington, D.C., as soon as—

SENTRY: There's no more room in the city for you people who don't have a place to live . . . *(To us)* Just then a wagon pulled up with friends of the sentry, who turned his back.

HANNAH *(Low)*: Jessa . . . you've got to keep down on the back of the wagon until you reach the other side. Find out where the president's house is, and I'll find you there.

JESSA: —What! No, Mama, don't leave me.

HANNAH: No slave catcher's going to catch up to you. Don't answer any questions from strangers . . . Just wait for me at the president's house. It's got to be the largest white plantation house in town.

SENTRY/CHORUS: And Hannah swept up Jessa and hid her in the back of the wagon under a burlap sack. The soldiers never noticed, and the driver cracked his whip, and off they went . . .

JESSA *(Peeking out of the wagon; softly, urgent)*: Mama!

HANNAH: The president's house!

Scene 16

AT THE WHITE HOUSE: "O TIDINGS OF COMFORT AND JOY." / THE PASSING OF THE STORY

Abraham Lincoln, Hay/Chorus, Nicolay, Ward Hill Lamon,
Louis J. Weichmann/Chorus, Members of the Cabinet and Company

CHORUS 1: And at that moment in the president's house, Mr. Lincoln was visited by his Cabinet and friends:

CHORUS 2: Mr. Seward, State.

CHORUS 3: Mr. Fessenden, Treasury.

CHORUS 4: Mr. Stanton, War.

CHORUS 5: Mr. Montgomery Blair, Postmaster General.

CHORUS 6: Mr. Usher, Interior.

CHORUS 7: Mr. Welles, Navy.

CHORUS 8: Mr. James Speed, Attorney General.

HAY: And Hay.

NICOLAY: And Nicolay served up the Christmas punch to all!

ALL *(Singing)*:

> God rest ye merry gentlemen, let nothing you dismay
> Remember Christ our Savior was born on Christmas Day
> To save us all from Satan's power when we were gone astray
> O tidings of comfort and joy, comfort and joy
> O tidings of comfort and joy.

CHORUS 4: The gentlemen in the room held only one opinion in common:

CHORUS 2: That never had they seen Washington more partisan, more conspiratorial than it was on that Christmas in 1864!

CHORUS 3: And in the gaiety, another figure entered the room so quietly that almost no one saw him come or go: Ward Hill Lamon, the president's Chief of Security . . .

LAMON: Mr. President: if I might have a word with you. *(The two withdraw)*

LINCOLN: Merry Christmas, Hill. If you don't quit on me again, I might have to promote you.

LAMON: I wish I could be merry, but it is an especially perilous time. I insist you be escorted for the next twenty-four hours.

LINCOLN: Have mercy! Surely conspirators and quacks celebrate the Yuletide, too!

LAMON: I don't ask to sleep outside your bedroom door tonight— which I think would upset the First Lady. But I must impose an escort around the clock.

LINCOLN: Even for the stroll to the War Department? I'll be with the others.

LAMON: Especially for the stroll to War. None of them could defend himself against an assault from any able-bodied woman in this city.

LINCOLN: You may escort me to the party at War. Meet me downstairs; we'll go over together. —Hill—take a glass of punch? Give us a song? Hill? Hill?

HAY/CHORUS: But Ward Hill Lamon had already vanished.

CHORUS 1: And Lincoln remembered his dream: for a moment he was on board a vast ship, racing towards a distant shore.

CHORUS 2: At the same moment, Nicolay remembered the letter about the widow Mary Surratt's boarding house but thought—

NICOLAY: Oh, it can wait until Monday . . .

(Hay and Nicolay toast each other.)

ALL *(Singing)*:

> God rest the ruler of this house and send him long to
> reign
> And many a Merry Christmas may he live to see again;
> Among your friends and kindred that live both far and
> near—
> May God send you a Happy New Year, Happy New Year,
> May God send you a Happy New Year.

(The Cabinet lines up to shake hands with Lincoln, then exits after their lines.)

SEWARD/CHORUS 2: The story was told, to the merriment of the Cabinet, of Lincoln's Christmas dilemma. *(To Usher)* "He'd rather face the Army of Northern Virginia with a pea shooter than face Mrs. Lincoln without a Christmas present!"

USHER/CHORUS 6: And Usher passed on the story to Blair.

BLAIR/CHORUS 5: Who passed on the story to Speed—

SPEED/CHORUS 8: Who promptly whispered it to Stanton—

STANTON/CHORUS 4: And Stanton, much amused, reported the story back at the War Department: "And so the poor devil has to ride himself out in this cold, back to the summer cottage . . ."

CHORUS 1: And so the story passed around with gales of laughter until it reached the ear of a lowly clerk in the War Department: a Mr. Louis J. Weichmann.

(A Chorus member whispers in Weichmann's ear; the two laugh.)

WEICHMANN/CHORUS: And Weichmann thought, What a funny story! He would tell it tonight to amuse John Wilkes Booth back at the widow Mary Surratt's boarding house on H Street.

Scene 17

AT MRS. KECKLEY'S. "STITCH, THOUGHT."
THE FIRST TIME SHE REALIZED SHE WAS A SLAVE

Mrs. Elizabeth Keckley, Little Joe, Mr. Burwell, Aggy and Company

CHORUS 1: And meanwhile, Mrs. Keckley bent over her fine sewing. She had left to the last an order for Postmaster Blair's grandson, a cloak fit for a prince.

CHORUS 2: Beautiful fur, with a silver lapel, and gold silk inside. It was hard to sew a robe for a little boy, and not think of one's own. Stitch, thought; stitch, thought.

(The Ghost of George Keckley, Mrs. Keckley's son, appears behind her. She does not turn around.)

KECKLEY: I can't be thinking of you now, George. I've got to put my hands to use.

CHORUS 1: And Elizabeth Keckley remembered the first time as a little girl she realized that she was a slave.

(A little boy with a cap comes in: Little Joe. There is a large scale, and Mr. Burwell waits for him, picks him up, and puts him on the scale.)

BURWELL: Here you go, Little Joe, up on the scale.

AGGY: Lizzie, leave the room!

BURWELL: Forty pounds, now at age eight! We can't call you little anymore.

(Mr. Burwell lifts Little Joe off the scale and gives him to a member of the Chorus.)

I want you to go with this nice gentleman, who's going to take you for a ride into town . . .

(Little Joe leaves, taken by the hand. Mr. Burwell turns to Mrs. Keckley's mother:)

Aggy! You tell Charlotte now to stop crying like that. She's still got four of her sons. Tell her to stop! We haven't had a decent meal in two days!

AGGY: I'll do my best, Master Burwell. But you know, she just lost a child.

(Mr. Burwell steams off. Aggy turns to a seven-year-old Lizzie.)

KECKLEY: Mama?

AGGY: —Now don't you start getting upset on me, too, Lizzie. The Master won't sell you.

KECKLEY: But, Mama, I'm two years older than Little Joe!

AGGY: He won't sell you if we put your hands to use. So starting today, your mama's going to teach you to sew . . .

(Aggy begins to demonstrate. Mrs. Keckley stops at the memory; then she bends back to her sewing with redoubled effort.)

KECKLEY *(Singing)*:
> Sew the collar
> Finish the hem,
> Try to find time for
> The child of Bethlehem.
> What child is this who laid to rest
> On Mary's lap is sleeping?
> Whom angels greet with voices sweet
> While shepherds watch are keeping?

Scene 18

WASHINGTON'S CENTRAL MARKET /
MRS. KECKLEY'S ROOM: MOTHERS AND "ORIGINAL JOY"

Mary Surratt/Chorus, Anna Surratt/Chorus, Walker Lewis/Chorus,
Mary Todd Lincoln, Mrs. Elizabeth Keckley,
Vendor and Company

CHORUS 1: Meanwhile, another mother went searching in the cold for Yuletide cheer: the Widow Mary Surratt and her daughter Anna.

(Mary and Anna Surratt walk to the market.)

MARY SURRATT: I am so worried about your brother John. He seems so distraught!

ANNA: The war is lost. Mr. Booth and Mr. Payne will drop by to visit him, and maybe they can lift his spirits.

MARY SURRATT: The greatest American actor of our time, John Wilkes Booth, in my parlor! We'll buy a specially good dinner—and, oh Anna, I know what—let's buy a Christmas tree for the parlor!

ANNA: We don't have money for trifles, Mother.

MARY SURRATT: Nonsense! How much can a little pine tree cost?

CHORUS 1: And so Anna and Mary Surratt quickened their steps to the Central Market in search of a tree.

ALL *(Singing)*:
> Sew the collar,
> Finish the hem,
> Try to find time for
> The child of Bethlehem.

(They hum under the next lines.)

WALKER/CHORUS: All year mothers scrimped pennies from their household accounts: and now they scurry to find gifts to gladden the faces of their children. For if there is such a thing as Original Sin, shouldn't there be Original Joy as well?

WOMEN *(Singing)*:

> What child is this who laid to rest
> On Mary's lap is sleeping?
> Whom angels greet with voices sweet
> While shepherds watch are keeping?

ALL:

> This, this is Christ the King
> Whom shepherds guard and angels sing
> Haste, haste to bring him praise
> The babe, the son of Mary.

KECKLEY: And the recently freed black mothers, crammed into alley shacks, sought to buy tokens with their hard-earned money. For on this night, all children are as loved as the Babe of Mary.

ALL *(Singing)*:

> Why lies He in such mean estate
> Where ox and ass are feeding?
> The King of Kings a glory brings
> Let loving hearts enthrone Him
> Raise, raise the song on high,
> Let singing fill the earth and sky
> Joy, joy for Christ is born
> The babe, the son of Mary.

(The Company becomes the Buyers and Merchants of Central Market, calling out:)

"Buy your hot chestnuts! Hot chestnuts!" "Sharpen your scissors and knives! Sharp for your Christmas goose!" "Extra, extra, read all about it!" "Peace on earth, goodwill to men!" "Boughs of holly! Deck the halls! Holly and the ivy! Deck the halls! Boughs of holly!"

(The two Marys find themselves face to face in front of the holly Vendor.)

MARY SURRATT: Excuse me—but where would I find a Christmas tree?

MARY TODD LINCOLN: That's exactly what I want to know!

VENDOR *(Shrugs)*: Boughs of holly?

MARY TODD LINCOLN: My good man—don't you have any Christmas trees? Can you tell me where I can find—

(The Vendor has turned his back.)

Oh! How rude!

MARY SURRATT: Oh, no one's selling them. We'll have to put up boughs of holly and a brave front.

MARY TODD LINCOLN: It would have been so nice to perk up the Blue Room . . .

MARY SURRATT/CHORUS: A year from now at her trial for the assassination of Abraham Lincoln, it will be said of Mary Surratt that she wouldn't hurt a fly. Almost blind, she couldn't see a fly, much less swat one. But Mary Surratt could sense the saddest-looking woman in front of her. *(Back to talking with Mrs. Lincoln)* We all need a little something extra this Christmas . . .

MARY TODD LINCOLN: Yes! It's so hard, this Christmas . . .

MARY SURRATT: And so many lost in this war . . .

MARY TODD LINCOLN: . . . And I cannot grieve in public the ones I've lost from my family and my hometown . . .

MARY SURRATT: May I ask, where is your hometown?

MARY TODD LINCOLN: Kentucky. And the losses have been so heavy!

MARY SURRATT: Oh, I know, from one Southern heart to another, we must be good to those we have left.

ANNA/CHORUS: Anna found her mother, arm-in-arm with—Anna could hardly believe her eyes!—arm-in-arm with the enemy! *(To her mother)* —Mother—excuse us a moment please . . . *(Anna takes her mother aside)* Mother! Do you have any idea with whom you are chatting? You are engaged with Mrs. Abraham Lincoln!

MARY SURRATT: Oh! Oh, dear . . . oh but Anna—she can't help her husband's actions, now can she? *(Mary Surratt goes back to Mrs. Lincoln)* I hope you find your Christmas tree . . . and . . . I wish you a . . . a Merry Christmas.

(Anna and Mary Surratt exit.)

MARY TODD LINCOLN: Merry Christmas, to you and yours! People are so nice! I should get out more often. Wait a moment—I think I know where we can buy a Christmas tree!

Scene 19

IN SURRATT'S PARLOR / LINCOLN ON A SILVER PLATTER

John Wilkes Booth/Chorus, John Surratt/Chorus, Lewis Payne/Chorus, Louis J. Weichmann and Company

CHORUS 1: And in that moment, back in Mrs. Surratt's parlor, three conspirators were drinking their way into Christmas oblivion.

SURRATT/CHORUS: John Surratt.

PAYNE/CHORUS: Lewis Payne.

BOOTH/CHORUS: And John Wilkes Booth. *(To his friends)* "I come to bury Caesar, not to praise him. The evil that men do lives after them. The good is oft interred with their bones, so let it be with Caesar." . . . I tell you, Surratt, when I strode to the footlights of the National Theatre that night, I could see the mole on his face! I was that close.

SURRATT: Why didn't you just seize him then, and leave me out of it!

BOOTH: Good Lord, that's madness to kidnap a president in front of an audience packed to the rafters!

SURRATT/CHORUS: And just then, that pesky little clerk, Louis Weichmann, came rattling in . . .

WEICHMANN: Mr. Booth! How delightful!

SURRATT: Mother's still at the market, Louis. I'll call you when supper's ready.

WEICHMANN: Oh—jolly good—remind me to tell you of the most amusing story about our hen-pecked president that I heard at the office today—

BOOTH: Pray do tell it now.

SURRATT/CHORUS: And so he did, down to the details of his riding forth this very night:

WEICHMANN: And the president said: "I'd rather face the Army of Northern Virginia with a pea shooter than face my wife without a present!"

BOOTH: Well told! Well told! May I suggest you dress for dinner, where you'll regale us again!

(Flattered, Weichmann exits.)

SURRATT: Give it up, Booth. We've tried three times to kidnap that Illinois buffoon. Enough.

BOOTH: The good Lord himself is giving us a Merry Christmas! Lincoln on a silver platter! Payne, go around to Wormley and hire a cart! Surratt, meet us out back with tarp and rope, and a good strong gag . . . We'll find a deserted spot to wait . . . and once we've seized our prey, you know the route south, down to our friends in Maryland:

(Booth and Payne sing to the tune of "O Tannenbaum":)

BOOTH AND PAYNE:
> Dear Mother, burst the tyrant's chain
> Maryland, my Maryland
> Virginia should not call in vain—
> Maryland, my Maryland

(Reluctantly, Surratt joins in:)

BOOTH, PAYNE AND SURRATT:
> She meets her sisters on the plain
> *Sic semper* tis the proud refrain
> And spurns the Northern scum again
> Maryland, my Maryland!

Scene 20

RAZ REACHES THE POTOMAC: "LOVE AT FIRST SCENT . . ."

Raz, Silver, Decatur Bronson, Rose, Mule and Company

Raz comes in, leading Silver. As the night turns colder, they both have doubts.

RAZ *(Singing)*:
> I put my knapsack on my back,
> My rifle on my shoulder
> I'm a-gone away to Shiloh.

Silver! I see campfires ahead! We've caught up with Mosby's Raiders!

CHORUS 1: But when they got close, Raz saw the fires were on the northern side of the Potomac where Sergeant Bronson was shoeing a mule.

53

(Bronson thinks of Rose. She hovers behind him as he tries to work.)

ROSE: There are two R's in "Marry" . . .

BRONSON: Rose, baby, I can't be thinking of you right now. I've got to put my hands to use. —Stop thinking, Bronson! My hands are useless! Shoe this mule!

(Rose hears something first. Alarmed, she wants to warn him, but vanishes.)

CHORUS 1: Raz stood very still on the southern bank opposite the smithy and made not a sound . . .

CHORUS 2: But Silver smelled the mule, and the mule smelled fine.

(Silver neighs; Bronson stops. He looks at the Mule, who is paying rapt attention.)

And the mule smelled the air, and that horse perfume smelled fine!

(The Mule brays.)

CHORUS 3: What did the horse and mule know of North and South? All they knew was that the night was cold, and they should be flank to haunch together in the hay . . .

CHORUS 1: It was love at first scent . . .

(Silver inhales, rich and deep.)

CHORUS 3: It was the love that dare not bray its name—

(But the Mule brays, amorously.)

And that was enough to wake up all the animals in the whole damn camp!

(The Company makes a cacophony . . . but perhaps a rhythmic, musical one.)

BRONSON: —Halt! Who's there?!

(Bronson swiftly moves for his rifle and readies it.)

Announce yourself!

(Lights up on Mrs. Keckley.)

Scene 21

IN MRS. KECKLEY'S ROOM / STREETS / WHITE HOUSE: "MRS. KECKLEY SEWED ON."

Jessa, Mrs. Elizabeth Keckley, Abraham Lincoln, Ward Hill Lamon and Company

CHORUS 1: And Mrs. Keckley sewed on, knowing the hour was growing late while a little girl walked on the streets of Washington.

(The Company hums "What Child Is This?" Lincoln and Lamon walk briskly toward the gala at the War Department, escorted by a Guard.)

LINCOLN: My dear Hill, any assassin smart enough to get me is smart enough to stay off the streets tonight . . .

(Lamon, in a foul mood, watches Lincoln's every step.)

LAMON: No assassin is getting you on my watch.

LINCOLN: You've become deluded about danger. You see it everywhere.

LAMON: That is because it is everywhere to be seen.

Scene 22

AT THE WAR DEPARTMENT GALA:
"THE HOLLY AND THE IVY." / LINCOLN ESCAPES

Abraham Lincoln, Ward Hill Lamon and Company

CHORUS 1: When the president and Ward Hill Lamon reached the gala at War, the rooms were crammed with guests. And the president served Hill a cup of strong punch with his own two hands.

LINCOLN: Drain the cup, Lamon! And after your thirst is quenched—give us a song!

(The Company calls out: "A song, a song," etc. Lamon holds up his hand for silence, and steps forth to sing:)

LAMON *(In a falsetto or countertenor)*:
  The holly and the ivy
  When they are both full grown,
  Of all the trees that are in the wood
  The holly bears the crown.

(Lincoln applauds prematurely; everyone stares at his faux pas; Lamon continues:)

  The holly bears a blossom

CHORUS 1: And during the next twelve verses of "The Holly and the Ivy," the president saw that not even a six-foot-four-inch man would be missed . . .

56

(Lincoln tiptoes out of the party, then hurries away, giddy as a schoolboy.)

LINCOLN *(In his best falsetto)*:
>The holly bears the crown.

Scene 23

THE WORMLEYS' SHOP:
"I MUST HAVE THAT CHRISTMAS TREE!"

*Mary Todd Lincoln, Frederick and Jim Wormley,
Guard and Company*

Lights up on the Wormleys' shop. Jim and Frederick sit at the counter, bored. It's slow on Christmas Eve. A pine tree, trussed, stands against the counter. The bell of the shop door rings. They leap to their feet as Mrs. Lincoln enters with her Guard.

MARY TODD LINCOLN: Young men . . . is this Mr. Wormley's shop?
>*(She sees the tree)* I must have that Christmas tree!

FREDERICK: Yes, ma'am, but we only have one and our papa said—

GUARD: Do you know who you are talking to? This is Mrs. Abraham Lincoln!

FREDERICK: Ma'am! Yes, ma'am!   JIM: Your Excellency,
                                    Mrs. President!

MARY TODD LINCOLN *(Pleased; to her Guard)*: Please take this tree to the White House . . . to the Blue Room . . .

(The Guard staggers under the tree. They exit, Mrs. Lincoln waving her hand. The shop bell rings.)

57

GUARD/CHORUS: And at that same moment that Mrs. Lincoln was stealing her friend Mrs. Keckley's tree, her husband was tiptoeing out of the White House stable like a teenager past curfew.

LINCOLN: Old Bob, come on boy . . .

(Lincoln leads a very old horse. The Wormleys' shop bell rings again; Mrs. Lincoln pokes her head back in.)

MARY TODD LINCOLN: And—oh yes—send the bill to me, not my husband. Merry Christmas!

(The Company assembles; Lamon is still onstage in his recital. They've all been drinking the punch. They are singing:)

LAMON:

> *O Tannenbaum, O Tannenbaum*
> *Du kannst mir sehr geffalen!*

CHORUS:

> *O Tannenbaum, O Tannenbaum*
> *Du kanst mir sehr gefallen!*
> *Wie oft hat nicht zur Weihnachtszeit*
> *Ein Baum von dir mich hoch erfreut!*
>
> *O Tannenbaum, O Tannenbaum . . .*

Scene 24

ON THE STREETS OF WASHINGTON, D.C.
"HOLD ON, SOLDIER, WE'VE ALMOST GOT YOU HOME."

Clara Barton, Moses Levy, Walt Whitman/Chorus,
Soldiers/Chorus and Company

A commotion cuts off the Chorus as Soldiers bear a stretcher through the aisles with a pale, thin man in tattered Union rags. Clara Barton bustles on and pushes the Chorus aside.

CLARA BARTON: Excuse me, please. Gentlemen, ladies, please clear the way. Coming through, please, clear the way to the ambulance.

CHORUS 1: There on the wharf, Clara Barton was stepping off a Union steamship.

CLARA BARTON: Please, please, clear the way, please, please, clear the way!

CHORUS 2: The steamship had boarded a gravely ill soldier who had escaped a Confederate prison.

CLARA BARTON *(To Stretcher Bearers)*: Please be careful of your step! —Can you back the horses down to the ramp?

CHORUS 3: Miss Barton kept the soldier alive on board ship, but his prospects looked dim. Walt Whitman once saw the arrival of starving prisoners of war. He wrote:

WHITMAN/CHORUS: "The sight is worse than any sight of battle-fields. There are deeds, crimes, that may be forgiven; but this is not among them."

SOLDIER: Miss Barton. Your patient is awake. *(To us)* The soldier woke on the trip only once—where was he? Was he dead?

SOLDIER/CHORUS AND MOSES LEVY: He found himself on the deck of some vast ship, racing towards a distant shore.

CLARA BARTON: Hold on, Soldier, we've almost got you home.

MOSES LEVY: Miss Barton? You don't remember me. I'm Moses Levy. You nursed me at Bull Run.

CLARA BARTON: I never forget a face.

MOSES LEVY: I am much changed since then.

CLARA BARTON: We'll get some good honest food into you! The ambulance is taking you to the Armory Hospital. Save your strength; I'll come by soon to see you settled in.

(The Soldiers carry him out.)

Scene 25

ACT ONE FINALE. STREETS / WHITE HOUSE / SURRATT'S HOUSE / EDWARD'S FERRY: "THE NIGHT WAS TURNING COLDER."

Decatur Bronson, Jessa, Mrs. Elizabeth Keckley, John Wilkes Booth, Lewis Payne, Mary and John Surratt and Company

CHORUS 1: The night was turning colder as Mrs. Lincoln rushed back to the White House to prepare her surprise. Mary Surratt returned to an empty parlor, while shopkeepers packed up their wares to close their stores. And on the streets of Washington, a child, a child, shivers in the cold. It's Christmas Eve, and for those who follow the German customs, it's almost time to trim the tree. We'll take an intermission, and if you decide to stretch your legs outside, bundle up. It's cold tonight.

(As the Company sings, each member bundles up against the cold. A spotlight comes up on Bronson, listening, holding his rifle. He goes back to his anvil and its rhythmic pounding of metal. Lincoln quietly walks his steed past the Guard. Jessa, in another area, walks

*the streets of Washington, D.C. Mrs. Keckley stops again with her
needle and thread, some strange feeling in her bones.)*

ALL:

> Not only green when summer's here,
> But also when tis cold and drear,
> O Christmas tree! O Christmas tree!
> Thy leaves are so unchanging . . .

*(Across the stage, dim lights come up on Booth, checking the ammunition
in his gun, and Payne with rope and tarp, waiting as John Surratt
carefully bundles himself up.)*

BOOTH *(Hissing)*: Johnny Boy! Hurry up—sometime before
Christmas!

(Church bells chime six o'clock.)

Act Two

Scene 26

JESSA ON THE STREETS OF WASHINGTON, D.C.

Jessa and Company

At rise, Jessa walks through the streets of Washington, D.C.

JESSA *(Singing)*:
    Follow the drinking gourd.
    Follow the drinking gourd.
    For the old man is awaiting to carry you to freedom . . .

—The sky's so bright here you can't see the stars!

(Just then, Washingtonians/Chorus bustle onstage in last-minute preparations for Christmas. Jessa is jostled in their midst.)

ALL *(Singing)*:	JESSA *(Trying to speak over singing)*:
Ding dong! Merrily	Excuse me, sir! Lady, can
on high	you help me, please?
In Heav'n the bells are	Lady—sorry to disturb, you,
ringing:	lady, but may I ask . . .
Ding dong! Verily	Oh! Sorry! I'm—could you
the sky	please—could you
	please— Sir— Lady—
Is riv'n with angels singing:	Ma'am—Mister? Mister—
Gloria, hosanna in excelsis . . .	

JESSA: Could you tell me where the president lives?

CHORUS 1: And as the temperature began to plummet, Jessa walked the streets of Washington. What marvels there were to see! Gas streetlights—

JESSA: —Brighter than the drinking gourd!

CHORUS 2: Had she turned around in that moment, she would have seen a great white plantation house across the street, where the president lived . . . but Jessa followed the crowd of soldiers, ladies and merchants through the streets away from Pennsylvania Avenue . . .

JESSA: Excuse me, sir, can you tell me where the president lives?

CHORUS 3: Back then people could just walk up to the White House, knock on the door, and demand to speak to the president. Back then, the People of the United States were very much the president's boss. Nowadays, if someone keeps asking where the president lives . . . call the police. *(To Jessa)* Walk south/southwest past Northern Liberties until you reach New York Avenue. Right onto I street, left onto 16th Street, and follow it to Lafayette Square.

JESSA: Thank you, ma'am. I'm gonna learn to read! So I can show Mama and she'll never get lost!

CHORUS 1: But she did know her left from her right, and so she started out . . .

JESSA: Left, right, left, right . . .

Scene 27

"STITCH, THOUGHT" #2: "WHOSE GIFT IS THIS?"
IN MRS. KECKLEY'S ROOM

Walker Lewis, Mrs. Elizabeth Keckley and Company

The Ghost of George Keckley hovers behind Mrs. Keckley.

CHORUS 2: And Mrs. Keckley tried to concentrate on her fine sewing, but her mind kept wandering off on its own . . . stitch, thought . . . stitch, thought . . .

(Pause. Walker knocks on the door, startling Mrs. Keckley.)

WALKER: Evening, I've come to pick up the delivery to the Blair house . . .

KECKLEY: Oh, Walker, I haven't finished it yet.

(Walker spies a wrapped present.)

WALKER: Then whose gift is this?

KECKLEY: Oh, no. I forgot to give it to Mrs. Lincoln. Where is my mind? It's the shawl I knit for the president . . . his old one is so worn, and he likes to wear one when he goes to the theater . . .

WALKER: I'll just drop it by the White House. The president should have his gift on Christmas Eve. When I bring the carriage to carry us to the home, we can stop by the Blairs on the way.

KECKLEY: —Oh, Walker, you are an angel!

WALKER: Will you tell that to my wife for me?

Scene 28

ON THE WASHINGTON, D.C. STREETS: "LEFT, RIGHT . . . NO, RIGHT! THEN A LEFT . . ."

Jessa and Company

CHORUS 1: And Jessa walked the streets.
JESSA: Left, right . . . no right! Then a left right, left, right . . .

(Jessa exits as two Union Soldiers march in with a large Christmas tree . . . left, right, left, right.)

Scene 29

THE WHITE HOUSE CHRISTMAS TREE / "MARY TODD LINCOLN HAD FOUR MOOD SWINGS."

Mrs. Lincoln, Union Soldiers 1 and 2/Chorus

UNION SOLDIER 1 *(Overlapping Jessa)*: Left, right, left, right . . .
UNION SOLDIER 2: Halt!
MARY TODD LINCOLN: A bit more to the right. No, a bit more to the right. A bit more!

(She contemplates.)

No. No. That's completely wrong. Bring it to the left, as far as you can . . .

(The two Union Soldiers in the Blue Room try to position the tree.)

UNION SOLDIER 1: Left, right, left, right . . .
UNION SOLDIER 2: Halt!

MARY TODD LINCOLN: Let's try it in the other corner . . . Oh, yes, yes, that's much better. Now put the ribbons on, evenly, evenly! Evenly starting from the top.

(The Union Soldiers start to decorate, ineptly; Mrs. Lincoln takes over.)

UNION SOLDIER 2/CHORUS: Mary Todd Lincoln had four mood swings: grief-stricken;
UNION SOLDIER 1/CHORUS: rageful;
UNION SOLDIER 2/CHORUS: remorseful due to her rages;
UNION SOLDIER 1/CHORUS: and cheerful. In fact, when she tried to be cheerful, she was cheerful with a vengeance.

(As Mrs. Lincoln sings, she begins to twist the ribbons around the tree with abandon.)

MARY TODD LINCOLN *(Singing ever faster—almost more than humanly possible):*
    God rest ye merry gentlemen, let nothing you dismay!
    Remember Christ our Savior was born on Christmas Day!
    To save us all from Satan's power when we had gone astray!

UNION SOLDIER 2/CHORUS: Today we would call it manic . . .

MARY TODD LINCOLN *(Singing):*
    Oh tidings of comfort and joy—comfort and joy!

(Her mood starts to swing the other way; with growing melancholy.)

    O tidings . . . of comfort . . . and . . . joy . . .

(As Mrs. Lincoln tries to decorate, a melancholic version of "God Rest Ye Merry Gentlemen" plays under. The Chorus hums.)

UNION SOLDIER 2/CHORUS: Oh, pity the First Lady! All her husband's virtues were his own, all of his faults were laid at her door. The White House was one big fish bowl, for all the world to see.

UNION SOLDIER 1/CHORUS: She and her husband had strategized, pillow to pillow, late in the Illinois nights, and now she was barred from all of his meetings. She was told to look pretty—

UNION SOLDIER 2/CHORUS: —She was criticized for looking pretty while soldiers were dying.

UNION SOLDIER 1/CHORUS: And she vowed, she would not lose her temper in public ever again!

MARY TODD LINCOLN: I honestly do not know what comes over me. It's like a fire sweeps over me, and I am just not myself. *(Struggling to be cheerful)* —Oh, I can't wait to see his face when he sees this tree! *(Singing:)*

O tidings of comfort and joy!

(Mrs. Lincoln steps back and sees her handiwork—it looks like spaghetti.)

UNION SOLDIER 1/CHORUS: And just then, a snippet of music from the War Department gala floated over the air, and Mary Todd Lincoln became aware of how empty, how full of echo the White House was. Mr. Lincoln would be carousing with his men, and late! Late again! Past their agreed time of nine o'clock. She did not want to stay alone, listening still for the sound of Willie's voice. —Stop, Mary, do not think of that tonight . . .

MARY TODD LINCOLN: Give him the gladness of my heart!—the gladness of my heart!— *(She suddenly, with resolve, calls to the Union Soldiers)* Will you please have my carriage brought 'round at once?

Scene 30

AT THE WORMLEYS' SHOP:
"THAT TREE IS FOR OUR FIRST LADY!"

James, Frederick and Jim Wormley and Company

CHORUS 1: And back at Mr. Wormley's shop, Frederick and James were about to go on another journey.

JAMES WORMLEY *(In a rage)*: You did what?!

FREDERICK: But, Papa! It was the First Lady!

JAMES WORMLEY: I don't care if it was the Queen of England! That tree is for Elizabeth Keckley! That tree is for our First Lady! I don't care how you do it, but you get that tree back, or you find one, and get it here on the double . . . Why am I wasting my money on college for the likes of you!

JIM: But, Papa—

JAMES WORMLEY: Out of my sight!

Scene 31

AT EDWARD'S FERRY, DECATUR BRONSON
AND CHESTER MANTON SAUNDERS COLLIDE

*Decatur Bronson, Chester Manton Saunders, Widow Saunders,
Black Recruiting Officer (Corporal Wills) and Company*

CHORUS 1: Out of sight for any sharpshooter, back at Edward's Ferry, Decatur Bronson lowered himself to the ground.

(Decatur Bronson readies his rifle, softly treading the ground. Enter Chester Manton Saunders, with a steaming mug of coffee. The two collide, and Bronson almost shoots Chester.)

BRONSON: Good Lord!

(Chester raises his hands, holding aloft the coffee cup.)

CHESTER: Don't shoot, sir! Private Chester Manton Saunders, bringing you coffee, sir!

BRONSON *(Carefully releasing the rifle's hammer)*: Don't you have the sense of a mule! You announce yourself loud and clear unless you want to get your head shot off! There are Mosby Raiders all around out here!

CHESTER: Yes, sir! Asking leave to give you some coffee, Sergeant.

BRONSON: The way you got the shakes, is there any left in the mug? *(There is, Bronson drinks)* Thanks, Soldier.

CHESTER: The lieutenant said I should ask you when you'd like your supper, sir!

BRONSON: Makes me nervous to have a white man sir-ing me.

CHESTER: They say in camp you ran heedlessly into enemy fire during battle! They say you'll get the Medal of Honor, Sergeant!

BRONSON: Say—I'll bet you're one of those Northern abolitionist fellows—am I right?

CHESTER: Yes, sir. Second Rhode Island, sir.

BRONSON: It's "Sergeant." If you're going to stay here and gab, help with the bellows. Put your hands to use.

(Chester grabs the bellows; Bronson watches him for a moment.)

So how did you end up here, fetching my supper?

CHESTER: I want to aid in the abolition of the most pernicious evil that has been a pestilence to free men! I want to help liberate men from the shackles of—

BRONSON: —Private Saunders, you are preaching to the choir.

CHESTER: Oh. Right. But how could I read my books when I could hear regiments forming for the front on the college green?

BRONSON: A college boy! That's why your speech is so pretty.

CHESTER: It took me a couple of tries to sign up. My mother was dead set against it, and everyone knows my mother . . .

BRONSON: Your mother has a temper?

CHESTER: Far worse than a temper. She has the saddest way of looking at you, so mild, so sweet, so afflicted . . .

(Spot on a middle-aged Quaker Woman, Widow Saunders, with sorrowful eyes, staring at Chester with the heartbreak that only a mother's eyes can cast.)

Oh! Even now I can feel her looking at me—it is the worst feeling in the world. But I went at last to the Congdon African Baptist Church:

BLACK RECRUITING OFFICER: Uh-uh. Nope. Go on back to your widowed mother, Chester. I'm not about to enroll her only son . . .

CHESTER: But Corporal Wills, sir! Everyone else has turned me down!

BLACK RECRUITING OFFICER: Besides, aren't you a Quaker? How's a Quaker going to pick up a rifle and shoot somebody to kill!

BRONSON: —A Quaker! I thought you folks were against all war!

CHESTER: We are! I am! But I want to support my country— *(Back to Corporal Wills)* Corporal Wills, sir! If you don't sign me up, I'm signing up in Massachusetts!

BLACK RECRUITING OFFICER: Oh Lord. Well, you got the right to die along with all of us. But maybe I got a way to save your skin. Sign your name on the rolls here . . .

(Chester signs. His mother, whose back has been turned, whips around in alarm.)

WIDOW SAUNDERS: Chester Manton Saunders! What has thee done!

CHESTER: And who filled my head with abolitionist creed? I was raised at her knee to bear daily witness to the divine spark in every man.

WIDOW SAUNDERS *(Singing)*:
> Come all you true friends of the nation
> Attend to humanity's call:
> And aid in the slave's liberation
> And roll on the liberty ball!

(Chester, seized with guilt, starts to march away with his regiment.)

CHESTER: Mother, I will write thee every day!

(A faint chorus of:)

WIDOW SAUNDERS *(Singing)*:
> And roll on the liberty ball, and roll on the liberty ball
> And aid in the slave's liberation and roll on the liberty
> ball!

(She disappears; a loud gust of wind.)

BRONSON: Huh—a fighting Quaker!

Scene 32

HANNAH REACHES THE WHITE HOUSE

Pendel/Chorus and Hannah

PENDEL/CHORUS: And, for a second, Hannah was unmindful of the cold: she had reached the White House!

(Hannah knocks; Pendel/Chorus becomes the Doorkeeper.)

What are ya doin', knocking at the president's front door?
HANNAH: Excuse me, sir, have you seen my daughter? She's small, wearing a blanket—

PENDEL/CHORUS: This is the north door: potentates and diplomats from dominions all over the globe use this door. And the American voter. Your people use the tradesmen's door on the south side.

HANNAH: Thank you, sir!

(Hannah runs off.)

Scene 33

"Lincoln Must Pass This Way." /
On the Road to the Summer Cottage

John Wilkes Booth, John Surratt, Lewis Payne and Company

CHORUS 1: And at that moment, away from the bright lights of the White House, on the outskirts of town:

BOOTH: Lincoln must pass this way. All roads lead to Rome.

SURRATT: Our supper is getting cold, and Mother, right this moment, is wondering where we have gone . . .

BOOTH: Now, you are to call the president over to the cart. Ask for help.

SURRATT: Why must I be the pigeon?

BOOTH: Because he knows my face, Surratt. He saw me play Mark Anthony. Call out for help when Payne gives us the signal. And Payne . . .

(Payne steps forward with a club, smiling.)

He'll never know what hit him.

Scene 34

WIVES AND RAIDERS

Decatur Bronson, Chester Manton Saunders, Mule, Widow Saunders, Second Lieutenant, White Officer, Mosby Raider and Company

CHORUS 1: Several horseshoes, and several stories later, back on the banks of the Potomac:

BRONSON: I shouldn't have left that day. We knew the rebs were in the area; seen them marching up to the fields North, and what goes North must come South. So I said: "Rose, darling, stay in the house. Stick to the house." And I went into town to find some balm for one of our horses—and suddenly I could feel the ground pounding from the Texans on retreat, heading for the river . . . I raced back from town. The turnpike was yellow smoke from their hooves on the dirt . . . and she was gone. Taken off our own front porch.

CHESTER: I am sorry.

BRONSON: And let me tell you, if I ever find the man that took her from me! . . . You want to join me? *(Bronson starts to laugh)* We'd make a team!

CHESTER: Me? I could never shoot a man.

BRONSON: What if you had the chance to shoot the man who stole your wife? That killed your mother?

CHESTER: I guess I would do what Mother would want me to do. I'd pray for him. For the Divine spark in every man.

BRONSON: I'd shoot him on sight. —Whatever are you doing in the infantry?

CHESTER: I'm not in the infantry. I'm a private with the quarter-master's staff.

BRONSON: You ride the supply line here? Surrounded by Mosby's Raiders?

CHESTER: Yup! And so there I'd be on the wagon, keeping the books: "Three hundred chickens, four hundred pounds of salt pork—"

WHITE OFFICER: —Men! Raiders ahead! Draw your guns.

(We now hear a commotion; rebel yells, gunshots, fighting, men groaning, triumphant yelps! Chester throws down his gun and raises a handkerchief. A ragged Mosby Raider comes on, sees Chester crouching, and steals his handkerchief.)

MOSBY RAIDER: Nice handkerchief. *(Blood-curdling rebel yell)* WOO-HOOO!

(Mosby Raider exits. The Widow Saunders reads her son's letter.)

CHESTER: "Dear Mother . . . spent another long boring day on the books; our accounts are somewhat short."

CHESTER AND WIDOW SAUNDERS *(Singing)*:
    We'll build us a temple of freedom
    And make it capacious within
    That all who seek shelter may find it
    Whatever the hue of their skin . . .

CHESTER: "And so the next week we started out with fresh supplies . . ."

WHITE OFFICER: Okay, men, mount up! Keep your eyes out! It is imperative to deliver the mules to Winchester—do not let the mules be taken!

(Sudden invasion; rebel whoops, chaos.)

Oh God, I've been shot! Unharness the mules!

CHESTER: "And so I took some mules into the gully to try and keep them . . ."

(Chester leads a Mule down into a gully.)

Shhh, steady, steady. Good boy. No one will find us down here . . .

(The same Mosby Raider appears, with gun drawn.)

MOSBY RAIDER: Hey, mister . . . nice mule.

(Mule looks anxiously at Chester; Mule looks at gun. Mule shakes from fear.)

CHESTER: My lieutenant gave me express orders . . .
MOSBY RAIDER: Let me give you another express order, then . . .

(The Mule leaps into Mosby Raider's arms.)

WOO-HOOOO!

(Mule and Mosby Raider elope.)

CHESTER: "Dear Mother: Another dull day, with only the mules for lively conversation . . ."

(The Widow Saunders, reading his letter, joins in the song:)

CHESTER AND WIDOW SAUNDERS:
    Whatever the hue of their skin
    Whatever the hue of their skin . . .

CHESTER: And so Washington sent us a new officer the next week from West Point.

(A panicked Second Lieutenant runs across the stage screaming:)

SECOND LIEUTENANT: RAIDERS! Draw your guns!

(Chester throws down his gun. The same Mosby Raider comes on and points the gun at him.)

MOSBY RAIDER: Your mule sends his regards. Now climb down the wagon. Give me yer jacket.

(Chester obeys.)

Now yer hat. Nice boots. How about yer suspenders?!

(Chester disrobes.)

Can't keep yer pants up without suspenders! Oh—nice socks! Yer mother knit 'em? Just my size! WOO-HOOO!

(Chester dresses as he writes his mother.)

CHESTER: "Dear Mother: Thee mustn't worry. I have not yet encountered a Raider. Thee mustn't believe anything thee reads in the *Providence Journal*."

CHESTER AND WIDOW SAUNDERS *(Singing)*:
　　We'll build us a temple of freedom
　　Whatever the hue of their skin . . .

(Widow Saunders exits with her son's letter in hand; Chester rejoins Bronson at the fire.)

Scene 35

BACK AT THE SMITHY / THE ROSE DUET

Decatur Bronson, Chester Manton Saunders, Rose and Company

BRONSON: You're a brave man, Saunders. Takes guts to be fired on and not return the fire.

CHESTER: I can't kill a man. But I can make sure he gets his supper. Well, tonight I can write Mother about meeting you! The first good news that's not made up . . .

BRONSON: Listen, do you think you could teach me some new words? I try to write some to my wife every day. When I find her, I'm going to deliver a stack of letters.

CHESTER: You know how to write?

BRONSON: Rose started teaching me. She said she wouldn't marry me unless I could write like a free man who could spell his own name.

(Rose appears from the shadows and leans over Bronson.)

You never saw a student so eager to learn!

ROSE: Now let me see you write it again . . . Decatur Bronson . . .

BRONSON *(Concentrating)*: "Bronson . . ." I hate B's.

ROSE: That's almost right; the B faces the other way.

BRONSON: Rose! I can't even get the second letter of the alphabet right!

ROSE: Practice. Patience. Make those strong hands dance with the pencil.

BRONSON: How do you spell the word "would"?

ROSE: "Wood" as in timber? Or "would" as in "would you"?

BRONSON: Why don't words have one sound! And one meaning for one word! "Would" as in . . . wait a moment—how do you spell "will"?

78

ROSE: W-I-L-L—

BRONSON: I love L's. *(Bronson writes with concentration)* Now read it.

ROSE: Will you—wait, there are two R's in marry. Think of all the words that sound the same: "Mary" as in the Virgin; "Merry" as in Christmas and then there's—

(Bronson hurriedly corrects his sentence.)

Will you marry me.

(Rose takes the pencil and writes; Bronson reads; Rose exits.)

BRONSON: Yes! She said yes! I'm writing her every day until I find her. And then I'm going to deliver those letters . . .

(Chorus of Soldiers enters behind Bronson as he sings:)

> There's a yellow rose in Texas
> That I am going to see
> No other soldier knows her—
> No soldier, only me.
> She cried so when she left me
> It like to broke my heart
> And if I ever find her,
> We never more will part.

BRONSON AND CHORUS OF SOLDIERS:
> She's the sweetest rose of color
> This soldier ever knew
> Her eyes are bright as diamonds,
> They sparkle like the dew.
> You may talk about your dearest May
> And sing of Rosa Lee
> But the yellow rose of Texas
> Is the only rose for me.

(Music under; a medley that turns into "Lo, How a Rose E'er Blooming.")

CHORUS 1: And on that Christmas Eve, every soldier over a campfire had visions of their Roses left behind: Rose their wives, Rose their mothers, Rose their daughters, Rose their sweethearts—how beautiful the sound of Rose, Rose, Rose—

(The Women of the Chorus come forward, circle in a dance, and sing:)

WOMEN:

> Lo, how a rose e'er blooming,
> From a tender stem hath sprung!
> Of Jesse's lineage coming,
> As men of old have sung.
> It came a floweret bright
> Amid the cold of winter
> When half spent was the night . . .

(The Women turn away; the Men of the Chorus sing; Bronson and Rose dance.)

MEN:

> Oh, now I'm going to find her,
> For my heart is full of woe,
> And we'll sing the songs together
> That we sang so long ago
> We'll play the banjo gaily
> And we'll sing the songs of yore—

(Rose breaks away; Bronson is alone once more.)

BRONSON:

> And the yellow rose of Texas
> Will be mine forever more.

(Chester says nothing. He picks up the bellows, as Bronson picks up his hammer. They start to work.)

Scene 36

Lights up on a quivering Raz, held from behind, a dirty knife at his throat, held by a raggedy Mosby Raider. Another stands to his front, wearing a hodgepodge of Chester's clothes. Silver looks on, alarmed.

MOSBY RAIDER 1: Kiss yer mama good-bye! I'm going to slit your throat, yer rotten Yankee spy.

MOSBY RAIDER 2: It'd be a waste of blood now, Duncan. *(To Raz)* What's your name, mister?

MOSBY RAIDER 1: He don't even have peach fuzz on his face.

RAZ: Raz Franklin, sir. Erasmus Franklin. I've come to defend my country and states' rights! I brought my horse . . .

(Silver denies this: "I'm not joining up with these raggedy-ass Mosby Raiders." The Mosby Raiders release Raz.)

MOSBY RAIDER 2: You run on home to your mama. Company D's disbanded.

RAZ: Disbanded?! But I want to join up!

MOSBY RAIDER 1: It's over. All we got left is our pride.

MOSBY RAIDER 2 *(Singing)*:
　　Three hundred thousand Yankees is stiff in Southern dust!

MOSBY RAIDER 1:
　　We got three hundred thousand before they conquered us

MOSBY RAIDER 2:
　　They died of Southern fever and Southern steel and shot

MOSBY RAIDERS 1 AND 2:

> I wish we'd got three million instead of what we got.

MOSBY RAIDER 1: Hey, wait a moment, Samuel. Maybe we should let him join up. This blanket's too small, and my fanny sticks out in the snow . . . the kid could sleep on the end, and keep my backside warm!

MOSBY RAIDER 2: Duncan, you're a darn genius! We c'n take turns in the middle. What do you say, kid?

RAZ *(Thinking fast)*: But uh, what is Christmas Eve without a Christmas supper? There's a Union supply depot down the banks, a mile or so—I'll bet I'm light enough to cross the ice. Am I joined up?

(The two Mosby Raiders look at each other; one draws the same dirty knife.)

MOSBY RAIDER 1: Kneel!

(Raz kneels. Mosby Raider 1 touches each shoulder of Raz with the flat of his knife.)

MOSBY RAIDER 2: Arise, Private.

RAZ: Gentlemen, it's an honor to serve with you! I'll be back with some chickens on the spit!

(Raz sings as he gallops off with Silver:)

> I put my knapsack on my back
> My rifle on my shoulder
> I'm a-gone away to Shiloh . . .

Scene 37

MRS. ELIZABETH KECKLEY'S ROOM /
THE WASHINGTON, D.C. STREETS

Mrs. Elizabeth Keckley, Jessa, Hannah and Company

CHORUS 1: And Mrs. Keckley put another log on the fire. She had not yet finished the silk lapel of the little Blair's cloak. Stitch, thought; stitch, thought . . . There was an odd feeling of dread in the pit of her stomach that she could not shake.
KECKLEY: Elizabeth Hobbs Keckley! Put your hands to use!

(Yet, Mrs. Keckley sits still, listening, alert. Then she sings as she sews. Jessa wanders onstage, wrapped in her blanket walking the streets. Mrs. Keckley stops again, and draws her shawl about her. On yet another part of the stage, a desperate Hannah searches the grounds of the White House, looking for Jessa.)

> There is a balm in Gilead
> To make the wounded whole
> There is a balm in Gilead
> To heal the sin-sick soul.
> Sometimes I feel discouraged
> And think my work's in vain
> But then the holy spirit
> Revives my soul again:

HANNAH AND MRS. KECKLEY:
> There is a balm in Gilead
> To make the wounded whole
> There is a balm in Gilead
> To heal the sin-sick soul.

(Jessa continues to walk in a circle as the clock chimes eight o'clock.)

CHORUS 2: There were a great many things people didn't know
in 1864 about disease. But they did know about hypothermia
then and all the symptoms:

CHORUS 1: shivering;

CHORUS 3: poor judgment;

CHORUS 4: confusion;

CHORUS 2: and Jessa was showing all the signs . . .

JESSA: I think I went around this circle before. How come they
got so many circles here?

KECKLEY *(Singing)*:
No one shall be excluded
The promises are true
You may be filled, oh
Hungry one   HANNAH *(Singing)*:
The table's spread for you   There is a balm in Gilead
There is a balm in Gilead.   There is a balm in Gilead.

(Jessa disappears offstage. Mrs. Keckley sews one last stitch.)

KECKLEY: There! It is finished!

Scene 38

IN THE WORMLEYS' SHOP:
"SERGEANT FREDERICK WORMLEY, REPORTING!"

Frederick and Jim Wormley and Company

Frederick and Jim Wormley dress in Union uniforms.

CHORUS 1: And back in town, the Wormley boys were about to go
on a journey of their own.

FREDERICK: How do I look in blue? Sergeant Frederick Wormley, reporting!

JIM: Our sister is going to kill us when she finds out we've stolen the uniforms she's sewing.

FREDERICK: We're just borrowing. *(Salutes)* Lieutenant Frederick Wormley, reporting!

JIM: I told you we should've closed up shop early!

FREDERICK: We would have lost money on the cart that Mr. Payne rented from us—

JIM: Can't we be arrested? For impersonating soldiers?

FREDERICK: Don't worry about it, 'cause we'll be shot for stealing White House property . . .

JIM: Damn. You look sharp, Brother. How about me?

FREDERICK: Suck in your gut, college boy. Throw your chest out. Look: General Frederick Wormley, reporting!

(Music up: "The Girl I Left Behind Me." Jim and Frederick in stiff military fashion march off as a veiled woman walks onstage.)

Scene 39

A WOMAN IN VEILS WAS MAKING HER ROUNDS AT THE ARMORY HOSPITAL

Mary Todd Lincoln, Moses Levy, Matron, Walt Whitman,
Henry Wadsworth Longfellow, Lieutenant,
John Wilkes Booth/Chorus and Company

CHORUS 1: And at that hour on Christmas Eve in the Armory Hospital, the men on Ward A were nestled, all snug in their beds. In the middle of the row, Moses Levy lay down his head, as a woman in veils was making her rounds in the ward.

CHORUS 2: Why did she keep her visits in secret? Was it her guilt at visiting Union soldiers, when her own family's Confederate members were slumbering with the slain?

CHORUS 3: What child is this who lays to rest on Mary's lap is sleeping?

(The woman sits down beside Moses Levy, and lifts her veils. It's Mrs. Lincoln.)

MARY TODD LINCOLN: Would you like me to get you a little stew? It will give you some strength . . .

MOSES LEVY: No, ma'am, thanks all the same. It's a waste of good stew . . .

(Moses Levy just manages to nod throughout the following.)

MARY TODD LINCOLN: We'll just have a little chat, then. My youngest boy is at the Blairs' house party, and I thought I might take a little time while my husband's out of the house. He's such a dear man, but I'll bet he's forgotten the time, and he's probably forgotten to shop! Not that I need anything, I have all I need: I have my health! And I have my husband . . . such a good man. Such a . . . a tall man! But he's like you, all skin and bones . . . and it's so funny . . . when he comes into a room . . . his knees don't know what his feet are doing, and his arms don't know what his legs are doing . . . so if there's anything fragile, anything breakable!—why, don't you know, somehow or other his foot finds it, or his elbow sweeps it off the table . . . A bull in a china shop, as they say—but such a good man!

MOSES LEVY *(Trying to keep up)*: What . . . what does your husband do?

MARY TODD LINCOLN: What does he do? He . . . he was trained as a lawyer. Yes! He taught himself to read, and don't you know, passed the bar on his first try . . . and you know how lawyers are . . . they never make up their mind about anything. You say to him: "Oh, just make up your mind! Free the slaves!" But it takes him months, years, and he argues it, and twists it around, and then finally—finally!—he does what is right, what you told him he should do, and he does finally, finally do it.

MOSES LEVY: He . . . sounds like a good man.

MARY TODD LINCOLN: Yes—that's it exactly! He's a good man. *(Suddenly conscious she is caring for a patient)* Oh, dear, here I am just chattering away . . . is there anything I can get you? *(No response)* No? Anything I can do for you?

MOSES LEVY *(Suddenly animated, sitting up)*: Can you find out where Walt is?

MARY TODD LINCOLN: Who?

MOSES LEVY: That funny poet fellow with the slouchy hat . . . Walt Whitman! I came through here maybe two years ago, with a bullet wound, and he came through the wards just about every night . . . he brings us things: trifles, but much desired—

(The Chorus of Patients steps forward.)

CHORUS 1: To me he brought an apple.

CHORUS 2: To me he brought a comb . . .

MOSES LEVY: I saw him sit with the most desperate cases . . .

CHORUS 3: My leg! The one that was amputated . . . it itched something terrible and I couldn't sleep. But Walt said that imagination was a terrible thing, and he sat with me through the night . . .

CHORUS 2: Walt didn't care where you come from, or what god you worship. He certainly didn't care who your bedfellow was . . .

MOSES LEVY: We think he's got some powerful magic. Maybe it's the poetry . . .

MARY TODD LINCOLN: You want a Mr. Walt? I'll go ask the matron when he'll be by . . .

(Mrs. Lincoln draws down her veils and goes to the Matron.)

MATRON: Whom? Whom do you seek?

MARY TODD LINCOLN: Walt Whitman?

MATRON: Walt Whitman? Whitman! God save me: Walt Whitman and Clara Barton and all the riff-raff who peddle themselves through these halls! Poets! Women! Bleeding-hearted do-gooders! A woman's place is in the home. In the hospital what is needed are staunch middle-aged women who can keep a stiff upper lip no matter the stench! —Walt Whitman! *(A smile breaks over her severe face; to Moses Levy)* Ah, yes. I regret to inform you that Mr. Whitman has taken ill, and has returned home to Brooklyn. *(Beat)* Good evening, madam.

MARY TODD LINCOLN: Oh my.

(Mrs. Lincoln goes back to Moses Levy.)

I am so sorry.

MOSES LEVY: Oh. Well. That's it for me, then. No. No. Thank you, ma'am.

CHORUS 1: For the past three years, Moses Levy found a minyan in the New York 40th Infantry: ten Jewish soldiers who could pray together. They improvised a seder each year, and celebrated the eight days of light. But in the Confederate prison, each man was alone to curse and pray for himself.

CHORUS 2: At least now, they could send his body home to his parents who would sit shiva for him, cover the mirrors, remember him living and pray for him dead.

MARY TODD LINCOLN: Is there anything? Anything else I can do for you?

CHORUS 3: And an involuntary moan escaped his lips.

(Mrs. Lincoln seizes his hand and holds it.)

MARY TODD LINCOLN: What would your mother do? Would she sing for you?

(Moses Levy nods. Mrs. Lincoln hesitates, then very softly, a capella:)

> Silent night, holy night
> All is calm; all is bright
> Round yon Virgin, mother and child
> Holy infant so tender and mild
> Sleep in heavenly peace.
> Sleep in heavenly peace.

MOSES LEVY *(With great effort)*: That's pretty. I don't know that song.

MARY TODD LINCOLN: You've never heard—? It's a Christmas carol.

MOSES LEVY: I'm Jewish.

MARY TODD LINCOLN: Oh! *(Having had let go his hand, she takes it again)* Oh . . . I don't know any Jewish songs. Shall I sing some more?

(Moses Levy nods. The Chorus steps forward and begins to sing the Kaddish. "Silent Night" sounds Middle Eastern.)

MARY TODD LINCOLN:	CHORUS:
Silent night,	*Yisgadal v'yiskadash sh'mei rabbaw*
Holy night,	*B'allmaw dee v'raw chir'usei v'yamlich malchusei,*
Shepherds quake	*B'chayeichon, uv'yomeichon*
At the sight . . .	*Uv'chayei d'chol beis yisroel . . .*

CHORUS 3: But already his fever was rising, a flood, taking him with it. And Moses Levy started to talk out of his head:

MOSES LEVY: Do not go. Your husband is wearing his new shawl. You must not let him go.

MARY TODD LINCOLN: Go? Go where?

BOOTH/CHORUS: In his delirium, Moses Levy saw himself carried up a narrow passageway to the box circle of Ford's Theatre:

MOSES LEVY: Someone has bored a hole in the door, and stands outside the Dress Circle. You are being watched through the door.

MOSES AND BOOTH *(Together)*: *Sic semper* . . . *(Shouting) Sic semper!* . . . *(Moving out of bed, Moses Levy starts to clutch Mrs. Lincoln's skirts)*

CHORUS 3: And Moses Levy's bedmate roused himself to come to her aid. —Hey, now, Soldier, easy, easy, there. Let go, Let go . . .

MARY TODD LINCOLN/CHORUS: And Mary Todd Lincoln saw the signs of the fever that had taken her young son.

CHORUS 3: You should leave now, ma'am. He's gone out of his head— *(Calling out)* Matron? Matron!

MOSES LEVY: You Sockdologizing Old Man Trap!

MARY TODD LINCOLN: Oh. Oh.

CHORUS 3: I'm sure he doesn't mean you, ma'am.

MATRON: You need to leave.

MARY TODD LINCOLN: Oh, let me stay. Perhaps—perhaps I could put my hands to use?

(The Matron has joined in the fray; they wrestle Moses Levy back into bed.)

MATRON: There's nothing you can do. —Lieutenant, grab his hands!

MARY TODD LINCOLN: Please, let me stay! I left Willie's bedside to go to the reception, in just such a state and he . . . I don't want to leave!

MATRON: Do you know your way out?

MARY TODD LINCOLN: Yes, yes, of course. I am so sorry. *(She tries to get composure; to the Lieutenant and the Matron)* Will you tell the young man that I will be back tomorrow?

CHORUS 3: He may or may not be here. But his body will be.

(Mrs. Lincoln veils herself and sweeps from the hospital.)

Scene 40

AT THE WHITE HOUSE DOOR: HANNAH'S CHOICE

Pendel/Chorus, Walker Lewis, Hannah, Slave Catchers 1–3,
Ward Hill Lamon and Company

CHORUS 2: And Walker Lewis had just delivered the new shawl that Mrs. Keckley had knit for the president. The doorman met him at the service stair:

PENDEL: Lewis. Come quick. One of your people is hammering at the front door, and she won't go away.

CHORUS 1: And so Walker Lewis arrived at the front door where he found:

(Hannah, shivering, in a panic.)

HANNAH *(Gripping him)*: I will not leave until I see the president! The president has to help me find my baby girl! My Jessa—

PENDEL: The president isn't here.

WALKER: I work for the president.

HANNAH: Oh God, sir, help me! My little girl! I can't find my baby!

WALKER: She's freezing. Let us sit inside for a moment.

PENDEL: No further than the porch. And be quick about it; Mr. Ward Hill Lamon has ordered us all to be on high alert—

WALKER: Okay, ma'am. Ma'am? You must calm yourself. And then start from the beginning.

HANNAH: I had no idea how big the town is! No idea, no idea! I sent my baby out in this town! In this cold! Jessa, Jessa, Jessa . . .

WALKER: I'm taking you inside . . .

(Walker takes off his coat and wraps Hannah in it. To Pendel:)

Please . . . she's half frozen.

(Pendel nervously lets them in.)

PENDEL/CHORUS: And so Hannah told Walker the story from the start . . .

WALKER: What time did you last see her?

HANNAH: The clock was striking five! I remember . . .

WALKER/CHORUS: And Walker calculated how long the girl could last in thin shoes, a dress and a blanket . . . four, five hours at the most. *(To Hannah)* Why did you put your daughter on the wagon without you?

HANNAH: I was scared that the slave catchers would catch up to us . . .

WALKER: Slave catchers! Good Lord, there aren't any slave catchers anymore . . . *(To us)* But Hannah had never been ten miles off the farm before. And only a short time ago, the slavers were thriving in Washington, D.C. . . .

SLAVE CATCHER 1: At your service. You can find me at John Beattie's Auction block on O Street . . .

SLAVE CATCHER 2: At Lloyd's Tavern at 7th and Pennsylvania.

SLAVE CATCHER 3: At Isaac Beer's Pen near the Center Market . . .

SLAVE CATCHER 1: At the biggest slave market anywhere: in sight of the White House,

SLAVE CATCHERS 1, 2 AND 3: The Slave Pen on the Mall.

HANNAH: No more slave catchers? Oh my God, what have I done . . .

CHORUS 1: And right then, an enraged Ward Hill Lamon rushed through the vestibule:

LAMON: Where the hell is the president! Someone must have seen him leave!

(He storms off.)

Scene 41

MEETINGS ON THE WASHINGTON, D.C. STREETS, PART 1:
"LINCOLN'S NOT COMING."

John Surratt, Lewis Payne, John Wilkes Booth, Jessa and Company

Across the stage, our three conspirators wait; Surratt stamps his feet. He takes off his gloves and blows on his fingers.

SURRATT: Booth. I'm cold. Aren't you cold?

(Booth just smiles.)

Lincoln's not coming. Let's just pack it in and head back to the boarding house. Mother must be out of her mind with worry.

BOOTH: Payne? Are you cold?

(Payne shakes his head no.)

Payne here says it's a balmy spring night. Here— *(Booth draws out a flask)* Drink up.

SURRATT: This is not a good idea. Mother must be—

BOOTH: —Good God! Are you a man or a mama's boy?

(Just then Jessa wanders onstage and sees the three men; she stops, scared. Booth notices her.)

—What the hell are you looking at? Git!

(Jessa runs. And runs. To the other side of the stage. She has dropped her blanket behind her. Now the wind comes up and she shivers . . .)

CHORUS 1: Jessa was now only two blocks away from the men in the dark who scared her, and it was hard now even to walk. There were no other people to be found on the streets. Her mother had asked her to . . . What had her mother asked her to do?

Scene 42

MEETINGS ON THE WASHINGTON, D.C. STREETS, PART 2: "ONE SOLITARY FIGURE ON HORSEBACK."

John Surratt, Lewis Payne, John Wilkes Booth, Jessa, Abraham Lincoln and Company

CHORUS 2: But to one solitary figure on horseback, the icy December air was a blessing . . .

(Lights up on Abraham Lincoln, enjoying a leisurely "ride" up 7th Street.)

CHORUS 1: The cold air felt so good knifing into his lungs; all the White House intrigue evaporated. The president looked up, and as the streetlamps got fewer and far between, he could see the winter constellations . . .

LINCOLN: It reminds me of riding the circuit in Illinois, when I was a young lawyer! Oh, how wonderful it feels to be free beneath the stars, and bundled against the cold!

CHORUS 2: And in the precious solitude, he started to work on his Inaugural Address as he rode, hammering out the words on the anvil of his mind . . .

LINCOLN *(To himself)*: Fondly, do we hope . . . fervently do we pray . . . that this great scourge? That this mighty scourge of war may speedily pass away . . . With malice toward none . . .

(From across the stage:)

SURRATT: I see someone coming . . .

BOOTH: Is it Lincoln? —Conceal yourself!

LINCOLN: . . . With charity for all, with firmness in the right as God gives us to see the right . . .

CHORUS 3: And then the lanky figure of the man passed beneath a streetlamp, closer now to Jessa, and she could see his face:

JESSA: Oh . . . oh . . . that man has the saddest face I ever saw.

LINCOLN *(On a roll now, oblivious)*: . . . Let us strive on to finish the work we are in, to bind up the nation's wounds . . .

CHORUS 2: And suddenly, Mr. Lincoln had a prickling sensation: someone was watching him . . .

CHORUS 1: And he looked down, and saw in front of him a little girl, in a thin calico dress, staring at him. And so he smiled, and lifted his hat to her . . .

CHORUS 3: And in an instant the president had passed by the little girl on the street.

(From across the stage; whispered:)

BOOTH: Get ready!

SURRATT *(To himself)*: Mother, I hope this will make you proud of me . . .

CHORUS 3: But in the middle of the next block, he thought:

LINCOLN: —What is a little girl doing out on the street this time of night? That child had no coat on in this cold!

CHORUS 1: And Lincoln turned his horse around and went back to Jessa.

CHORUS 2: And again, he lifted his hat:

LINCOLN: Good evening, miss. Are you all right? Do you live around here?

CHORUS 1: And in confusion, Jessa tried to remember what her mother had said.

LINCOLN *(Kindly)*: Do you need help? Where is your mother? Your father? *(He waits)* Are you lost?

JESSA *(With dawning horror)*: Slave catcher!

CHORUS 1: Jessa willed her feet to fly . . . and she ran through the streets to keep the blood warm, ran until she ran out of breath . . .

BOOTH: Surratt? What's happening? Can you still see him?

SURRATT: He turned his horse around. Wait.

Scene 43

MEETINGS ON THE WASHINGTON, D.C. STREETS, PART 3: "THE CONSPIRATORS NEVER RENTED THE WORMLEY HACKS AND HORSES AGAIN."

John Surratt, Lewis Payne, John Wilkes Booth/Chorus, Abraham Lincoln, Frederick and Jim Wormley and Company

CHORUS 1: Right then, Frederick and James Wormley rattled on in their cart.

BOOTH: Damn. Union soldiers!

(Frederick and Jim see the cart.)

FREDERICK: Hey! That looks like one of our carts! That customer didn't return it . . . *(Calling)* That's our cart!

SURRATT *(Alarmed)*: They're on to us!

JIM: Mr. Payne! Is that you, Mr. Payne?!

BOOTH: You gave them your real name? Idiot! Disperse—meet back at the boarding house—

(The conspirators disappear. Frederick and Jim catch up to the now empty space.)

JIM: Man! Look at them run!

FREDERICK: We'll tell Papa later . . .

CHORUS 2: The conspirators never rented the Wormley hacks and horses again.

BOOTH/CHORUS: Booth gave his patronage from that night on to a stable conveniently close to Ford's Theatre.

Scene 44

AT THE WHITE HOUSE GATE: "SHE'S BEEN ON US ALL NIGHT ABOUT THAT TREE . . ."

Frederick and Jim Wormley and Sergeant-at-Arms

FREDERICK: Okay. One more time. What are you going to say to the Sergeant-at-Arms when we get to the White House?

JIM: Sir! We're here on orders from the president himself!

FREDERICK: No, Brother! The second you say something like that, that soldier's going to ask for your papers. Why would the president bother with the likes of us?

JIM: All right, then. You're so smart—what do you propose?

FREDERICK: We've got to appeal to a higher power.

(The Wormley boys appear in front of the Sergeant-at-Arms.)

SERGEANT-AT-ARMS: Halt. Present your papers and your business . . .

FREDERICK: Yes, sir. We're here on the order of Mrs. Abraham Lincoln, who told us to be quick about it: she wants us to bring her the Christmas tree immediately . . . wait a moment, let me find my papers, they're somewhere on me . . .

SERGEANT-AT-ARMS: Go! Go! Get the darn thing . . . she's been on us all night about that tree . . . just take it, take it! It's in the Blue Room!

JIM: Yes, sir!

FREDERICK: On the double, sir!

(Frederick and James approach the tree, and take it. With their best military bearing, they march it from the White House.)

Scene 45

OUTSIDE THE WHITE HOUSE:
"WE'RE GOING TO FIND HER. I GIVE YOU MY WORD."

Walker Lewis, Hannah, Pendel,
Frederick and Jim Wormley and Chorus

CHORUS 1: And as the Wormley brothers secured a much-trafficked Christmas tree in their cart, they saw Walker Lewis hurrying a woman along:

WALKER: Frederick! Quick! Wrap this woman in your blankets . . . *(Hannah gets covered. To Hannah)* Now listen, ma'am, you've got to get off the streets. These gentlemen will deliver you to a Mrs. Elizabeth Thomas and my wife in Georgetown—to the Cox House . . . if anyone in our community has found Jessa, that's where they'd take her.

HANNAH: No, no, I've got to find my baby, my Jessa.

WALKER: We're going to find her. I give you my word. Yes?

HANNAH: You give me your word?

WALKER: That's right. My word. We've got friends who know every alley and every side street. —Frederick, how many carts can your father spare?

CHORUS 1: And before you can say "St. Nicholas," they got that shivering mother on the seat between them, and off they rode down the cobblestone streets to the Cox House and Mrs. Thomas . . .

Scene 46

ON THE WASHINGTON, D.C. STREETS:
"WHO KNEW THAT FREEDOM WOULD BE SO COLD?"

Jessa and Company

CHORUS 1: Jessa was in a part of town where the lights were brighter, and a few stragglers were on the street. They passed her, without seeing her, and she didn't even try to talk.

ALL *(Distantly, a ghostly song)*:
  Ding-dong merrily on high . . .

JESSA: Oh. Tonight is my first night of freedom.

ALL *(Singing underneath)*:
  In Heaven the bells are ringing.

CHORUS 2: Who knew that freedom would be so cold?

CHORUS 1: She walked midway down an alley sheltered from the wind. And down in the alley, she saw a big open crate with straw, which someone had thrown out with the trash. It looked like a little stable in a box. It would be warmer than the streets, and she was just small enough to crawl inside . . .

Scene 47

"INSIDE THE LINCOLN WHITE HOUSE THERE LIVED AN AFRICAN VILLAGE."

Walker Lewis, Philip Reid/Chorus, Mrs. Johnson,
Reverend Wallace Brown, Elder Anthony Bowen,
Mrs. Elizabeth Thomas and Company

CHORUS 1: The clock struck nine. At ten o'clock every free person of color had to be off the streets: ten o'clock, and curfew.

WALKER: Not many historians write about it, but inside the Lincoln White House there lived an African village: the basement of the house, where the cooks and the messengers, the seamstresses and the staff lived. The White House kitchen—where right now, there was a party going on.

(Music and dancing: the Company celebrates Christmas in the kitchen. Walker rushes inside the kitchen.)

People! Good people! I need your help!

CHORUS 1: Any free person of color living in Washington, D.C., knew the adage by heart:

CHORUS 2: The president can't help us: he's too busy fighting the war!

CHORUS 3: The governors won't help us: it's not their jurisdiction!

CHORUS 4: The mayor won't help us . . . Hey, has anyone seen the mayor?!

CHORUS 1: God Helps Those . . .

ALL: who Help Themselves!

CHORUS 5: On cold nights like tonight, if someone lay down to sleep in the alley, they won't wake up in Washington, D.C.

CHORUS 2: Those poor souls will wake in the Promised Land.

WALKER: We've got to find that girl.

(First verse, "Children, Go Where I Send Thee." As the Black Chorus sings, they form bands with lanterns and, if there are local children in the production, they wrap the children in blankets and carry them off.)

BLACK CHORUS:

Children, go where I send thee
How shall I send thee?

WOMEN:

I'm gonna send thee one by one

MEN:

One for the little bitty baby

ALL:

Who was born, born, born in Bethlehem . . .

WALKER: Each of us runs to a church and calls out the elders . . .
How many folks do we have? Mr. Philip Reid!

REID/CHORUS: I am the man who cast the bronze Statue of Freedom, sitting astride the Capitol Dome.

WALKER: Mrs. Johnson!

MRS. JOHNSON/CHORUS: I'm the nurse who tends to the staff.

WALKER: Will you two kindly run to St. Paul's and call on the Reverend Wallace Brown.

(As the two leave and journey, they sing, and are met by Reverend Wallace Brown. With lanterns, they search the streets.)

ALL *(Singing)*:

Children, go where I send thee
How shall I send thee?

WOMEN:

I'm gonna send thee two by two

MEN:

    Two for Paul and Silas

ALL:

    One for the little bitty baby
    Who was born, born, born in Bethlehem . . .

WALKER: William Slade, the messenger; Peter Brown, the butler; the White House seamstresses, Mrs. Rosetta Wells, Mrs. Hannah Brooks: please run to the Second Colored Wesleyan, and call out Elder Benjamin Grant.

ALL *(Singing)*:

    Children, go where I send thee
    How shall I send thee?

WOMEN:

    I'm gonna send thee three by three
    Three for the Hebrew children

MEN:

    Two for Paul and Silas

ALL:

    One for the little bitty baby
    Who was born, born, born in Bethlehem . . .

WALKER:

    Children, go where I send thee
    How shall I send thee?
    I'm gonna send thee four by four
    Four for the four who stood at the door . . .

(Members of the Company may deliver children to the Cox mansion, where Mrs. Thomas waits.)

CHORUS 1: And they wrapped the children they had found in swaddling blankets and dropped them on the doorstep of the Cox House in Georgetown, where an anxious Mrs. Thomas kept watch.

MRS. THOMAS *(Singing)*:
    Children, go where I send thee!—

(She looks; there's not an inch of space.)

Where shall I send thee? *(To us)* My name is Elizabeth Thomas. Lately I've had to live with my daughter and her husband here in Georgetown . . . so I come and help at the Home for Destitute Women and Children. But don't you call me destitute! I had a good home until the government came along, talking "eminent domain"—they said they had to pull it down and build a fort. I said: "This is my domain, the domain of Elizabeth Thomas!" But they pulled down every two-by-four and used it for the fort. Fort Stevens! But they left the front steps where they were. And so when the weather's nice, I go and sit on those steps, just like I have for the past twenty years. So I was there, sitting on my own front steps, when suddenly rebel soldiers poked over the hill and started firing on Fort Stevens . . . and shells and miniballs and all kinds of metal starts winging over my head, and I thought I'd better get out of there. And I look up, and see this lean, lanky white man, dressed in black, with a big stovepipe hat, standing up high at the front of the fort! So I yell: "Tell that fool to duck his head down!" And that's how I saved President Abraham Lincoln of these United States . . . I said! Abraham! *(Singing:)*

    Child, go where I send thee!
    How shall I send thee?
    I'm gonna send thee five by five
    Five for the children who started to jive . . .

CHORUS 1: And so they ran:

(Singing:)

    Some to the Shiloh Baptists;

CHORUS 2:
    Some to the Ark, Mount Zion;

CHORUS 3:
    Some to Ebenezer United;

WALKER:
    Some to the Fifteenth Street Presbyterian!

(Walker suddenly realizes the kitchen is empty.)

Oh Lord! Mrs. Keckley!

(And he sprints. Lights up on Mrs. Keckley and Walker.)

ALL *(Softly singing/overlapping):*
    Children, go where I send thee.

Scene 48

AT MRS. KECKLEY'S ROOM: "I'M GOING WITH YOU."

Walker Lewis, Mrs. Elizabeth Keckley and Company

KECKLEY *(Pulling on coat, gloves and hat, singing):*
    I'm going with you.

ALL *(Singing):*
    Children, go where I send thee . . .
    (Repeats)

WALKER: Mrs. Keckley, it's cold outside. Fifteen degrees and falling . . .

KECKLEY: I don't care. What was she wearing?

WALKER: A calico dress. Some raggedy shoes . . . and a blanket.

KECKLEY: Let's go.

ALL *(Singing)*:
> Children, go where I send thee . . .

Scene 49

ON THE BANKS OF THE POTOMAC:
"SILVER! I'LL BE BACK . . ."

Raz and Silver

Raz ties Silver to a tree.

RAZ: Okay, Silver, I'm leaving you way down the bank . . . downwind of those Union mules so you can't flirt with them across the river . . .

(Silver silently pleads: "Don't go . . .")

Look, if I don't go, I can't come back with corn and hay . . .

(Silver: "I don't care . . . Don't go . . .")

I'll be back before you know it. Just stay here and wait for me . . .

(Silver grabs Raz's coat sleeve with her teeth.)

Silver! Silver! I'll be back before you know it . . .

(Raz pries Silver's teeth from his sleeve. Then he lowers himself onto the ice of the Potomac . . . tests it gingerly with his weight, and slowly crosses the ice. Silver watches from the bank, giving one short, soft neigh.)

Scene 50

AT THE ARMORY HOSPITAL: MOSES LEVY IS VISITED BY ST. NICK (OR WALT WHITMAN?)

Moses Levy, Walt Whitman and Company

CHORUS 1: And back on his hospital cot at the Armory, Moses Levy was getting ready to cross one more river himself. But a soft noise woke him. Someone was walking down the row of beds.

(Lights up on Moses Levy. A costumed, bearded man, dressed as St. Nicholas, stops at each bed, leaving small gifts on each table.)

CHORUS 3: To me he brought a comb;
CHORUS 4: to me he brought a handkerchief;
CHORUS 2: trifles, but much desired . . .
CHORUS 1: The man stepped into a shaft of moonlight, and Moses saw:
CHORUS 2: He might have seen a fantasy born of his fever . . . but I, myself, think he saw a kindly old gent, making his annual rounds: St. Nicholas himself. But did you ever notice? St. Nicholas bears a striking resemblance to:
MOSES LEVY: Walt!

(St. Nicholas lays a finger on his lips; smiling, he comes to Moses.)

CHORUS 1: And the old gent sat down beside Moses Levy, and took the young man's hand in his. And Moses drifted off to

106

sleep, smiling, knowing someone would be watching over his bed the whole night through . . .

Scene 51

At Edward's Ferry: Raz Is Taken Prisoner

Decatur Bronson, Raz, Chester Manton Saunders,
Black Union Soldiers and Company

CHORUS 3: And on the other side of the Potomac . . . the northern side . . .

(Lights up on Raz, seated on a tree stump, a rifle pointed at his head by Bronson, while Chester looks on in alarm.)

BRONSON: What the hell were you doing with your rump sticking out of the supply tent, your pockets filled with hardtack and your hands carrying hay?

RAZ: Look: it's Christmas Eve. My horse is starving. And my comrades are starving, too.

CHESTER: Comrades?

(Chester and Bronson examine Raz carefully under a lantern.)

He's younger than any freshman I ever saw at Brown University . . .

RAZ: I can whup any soldier, one on one in the Union Army! We'd have won this war if you hadn't of used bully tactics, picking on poor defenseless women and starving children of their bread.

CHESTER: You're too young to do much except play with a toy drum.

RAZ: You're talking to an enlisted man in Company D! Mosby's Raiders!

107

BRONSON: Oh God.

CHESTER: Then you owe me my jacket. You owe me my boots. You owe me my socks—my mother knit them. My name is Private Chester Manton Saunders. I am taking you prisoner.

BRONSON: No, we don't want to do that . . .

(From the shadows, two Black Union Soldiers enter.)

BLACK UNION SOLDIERS *(Whispering)*: Take no prisoners, take no prisoners . . .

BRONSON *(Low, to Chester)*: Private Saunders . . . I want you to walk back to the camp, very slowly. Very slowly. Do not tell anyone what has happened here. No one. Least of all the lieutenant.

CHESTER: What are you going to do, sir?

BLACK UNION SOLDIERS *(Feverish)*: Take no prisoners; take no prisoners . . .

BRONSON: You don't have to be around to see me break army procedures with a combatant . . . I'm going to release him.

CHESTER *(Relieved)*: I don't know anything about it.

BRONSON *(To Chester)*: Go now.

CHESTER: Yes, Sergeant!

(Chester salutes, and briskly leaves. A pause. Raz grows nervous.)

BLACK UNION SOLDIERS: Take no prisoners; take no prisoners . . .

RAZ: What—what's happening?

(Bronson, with his back turned, readies his rifle; he turns to Raz with his rifle raised, and aims at Raz's head.)

BRONSON: I'm sorry, son . . .

Scene 52

LOOKING FOR JESSA ON THE WASHINGTON, D.C. STREETS:
"WE HAVE TO ABANDON THE SEARCH."

*Mrs. Elizabeth Keckley, Walker Lewis, Philip Reid,
Reverend Alexander/Chorus and Company*

The Black Chorus gathers in the streets.

KECKLEY: Where is she? Where is she, where is she?

WALKER: Anybody? Any luck? Reverend Alexander? Mrs. Johnson?

MRS. JOHNSON: No. No luck. We asked everyone we saw; no one's seen a little girl.

REVEREND/CHORUS: We are praying for her.

(Right then the clock strikes ten.)

The bells are ringing curfew. We'd better get off the streets ourselves.

WALKER *(To Mrs. Keckley)*: We have to abandon the search. But . . . I gave her mother my word . . .

KECKLEY: You'd best tell her mother in person.

WALKER: Why don't you warm yourself by your fire; I'll get the carriage ready . . .

Scene 53

IN MRS. KECKLEY'S ROOM. A DREAM, A MEMORY:
"SHE WAS OVERCOME BY SLEEP . . ."

*Walker Lewis/Conductor, George Keckley, Mrs. Elizabeth Keckley,
Minister Bingham, Ghost of George Keckley and Chorus*

CHORUS 1: And as Mrs. Keckley sat down by her fire, she was overcome by sleep in her rocking chair.

(Walker changes into a Conductor at Union Station.)

WALKER/CONDUCTOR *(Echoing)*: I'll get the carriage ready . . .

All aboard! The 10:05 train to Ohio is now boarding on Track One . . . Next stop: Wilberforce! Wilberforce, Ohio!

(Mrs. Keckley fusses over George's coat and scarf.)

KECKLEY: You'll be the best-dressed undergraduate at Wilberforce College!
GEORGE *(Irritated)*: I'd rather wear the Union blue . . .
KECKLEY *(Alarmed)*: This is the white man's war; let them fight it out . . . tell me you'll stop this foolishness . . .
GEORGE: Don't worry. I'll be back at Christmas . . .

(Mrs. Keckley shudders as George hugs her and starts to leave. As he disappears in the light, we see a white, middle-aged Minister in the background, rolling up his sleeves, whip in hand.)

I'll be back at Christmas . . . *(He waves)* I'll be back at Christmas . . . I'll be back . . .
KECKLEY: I can't believe the daughter of a slave is sending her son to college—

(George is gone. The white Minister, in a clerical collar, approaches Mrs. Keckley, a short whip tucked under his arm.)

MINISTER: You have too much pride for a slave. Girl, take off your dress. *(Rolling up his sleeves higher)* Girl, take off your dress.
KECKLEY: No!
MINISTER: Girl, take off—
KECKLEY: No! You have no right! You do not own me! I will not! *(As he disappears into the shadows)* You could beat me, oh God, but look! Look where I am now!

110

(She tries to call him back to triumph over him.)

Look!

(A shadow, a figure of a man stands beyond her vision. She feels him there. The Ghost of George Keckley, in a Union tunic, holds a rifle aimed at the Minister. George is in battle, distant.)

George?
GEORGE: Mother?
KECKLEY: I should never have told you that story.
GEORGE: Mother?
KECKLEY: I should never have told you that story. George . . .
GEORGE *(A whisper as he is shot)*: Mama?!—

(Mrs. Keckley bolts upright at the sound of her son in danger. Surprise and realization spread on George's face as he sinks to his knees. Beat.)

KECKLEY *(Wide awake from her dream)*: I've got to get some air.

(Mrs. Keckley stands, takes her robe and walks into the alley.)

Scene 54

IN THE ALLEY: THE CRATE THAT CARRIED THE SILKS
Walker Lewis/Chorus, Mrs. Keckley/Chorus and Jessa

KECKLEY/CHORUS: And I walked down the back stairs and out into the alley. It was fearfully cold, and I saw something strange . . . there in the alley was the crate I'd thrown out, the crate that carried the silks from France to my doorstep . . . it looked like someone had thrown rags out in that crate, and so I looked:

111

(Mrs. Keckley reaches into the straw, and finds a little girl's foot with thin shoes . . . she tears through the straw and lifts out Jessa.)

WALKER! WALKER!!!

WALKER/CHORUS: And Walker Lewis picked that little girl up and put her in the carriage and he spurred on the horses.

KECKLEY: Quickly—to Mrs. Thomas!

WALKER/CHORUS: Yah! Mrs. Keckley bundled that little girl in a robe of silver and gold, fit for a prince . . . And as Walker urged the horses to clatter through the streets, Mrs. Keckley rubbed Jessa's cold hands, and she rubbed those icy feet, and she rocked that child and sang: Yah!

KECKLEY *(Singing)*:

> Mary had a baby
> Born in Bethlehem
> Every time that little baby cried
> She rocked him in a weary land
> Ain't that a'rocking? All night
> Ain't that a'rocking? All night
> Ain't that a'rocking—all night—
> All night long . . .

Come on, Jessa. Come on, baby girl . . . open your eyes . . .

WALKER: I'll spur the horses faster . . . Hold on.

Scene 55

EDWARD'S FERRY: "I DON'T OWN ANY SLAVES! I WORK IN A STABLE."

Raz, Decatur Bronson, Chester Manton Saunders/ Chorus and Company

We hear the click of a rifle hammer engaged. Lights up: Bronson aims the rifle at Raz's head. He squints, taking true aim . . . then lowers the rifle.

Taking paper and pencil from his jacket, Bronson lays them on the ground near Raz. We hear the Chorus softly sing "Take No Prisoners."

BRONSON: Hold on. The least I can do is make sure your body is returned to your parents. Write down your name and your address.

RAZ: I can't. I don't know how to write. My name is Erasmus Franklin . . . Raz.

BRONSON: What do you mean you don't know how . . . a young boy with money enough to own his own horse—what kind of a slave owner doesn't know how to write?

RAZ: I don't own any slaves! I never went to school. I work in a stable. I sleep in a stable. And now I'm about to be shot by a slave.

BRONSON: I'm as free a man as yourself. Paid for my own blood with my own hands. A free man has to keep his word. Even if I have to walk across a bridge of bodies all the way to Richmond. I'll make this quick; you won't feel it for long. Turn your head away, son.

RAZ: I would gladly spill every drop of my blood if it . . . if it would save my country . . . But could you just . . . give me a moment?

(Bronson nods. Raz faces away from Bronson, turning his head toward the south bank. Raz bows his head in a brief prayer, and says good-bye to the Shenandoah.)

CHESTER/CHORUS: And as he strolled back towards the campfire, Chester stopped, and he felt a strange feeling in his bones. There was more than one meaning to the word "release." And where he stood, Chester knelt and sent up a prayer to the Divine spark in every man.

RAZ: All right. I'm ready now . . .

Scene 56

THE WASHINGTON, D.C. STREETS / EDWARD'S FERRY: "TOGETHER THE TWO CHILDREN WHISPERED: 'MAMA.'"

Walker Lewis/Chorus, Mrs. Elizabeth Keckley, Jessa, Raz, Decatur Bronson and Company

WALKER/CHORUS: Through the streets, the horses raced on cobble-stones. —Any sign, Mrs. Keckley?

KECKLEY: God, no. She is ice . . . She is stone—God, oh God!

CHORUS 1: And Mrs. Keckley opened her coat.

CHORUS 2: She opened her dress.

CHORUS 3: And she drew that child onto her breast.

(Mrs. Keckley shudders at the coldness of Jessa's skin.)

CHORUS 4: Her own skin felt like a torch on ice.

CHORUS 5: And she rocked;

CHORUS 6: and she rubbed;

CHORUS 7: and she urged that child to breathe:

KECKLEY *(Singing)*:

> Herod hear of the news
> Baby he did seek
> Lord told Mary,
> "Just you rock him in a weary land . . ."

(There is another gust of wind: the Ghost of George Keckley behind Mrs. Keckley. He holds out his arm for Jessa's body. Mrs. Keckley sees him.)

George, I promise I will let you go—just give me back this child—

ALL *(Singing)*:
>Ain't that a'rocking? All night
>Ain't that a'rocking? All night
>Ain't that a'rocking—all night—
>All night long . . .

(Raz and Bronson stand still. Slowly, Bronson raises his rifle again, and aims.)

CHORUS 1: The night would not be long enough for a boy who pretended to be a soldier. And at the exact same moment that Raz drew his last breath, and tried to die a brave man, he closed his eyes just as Jessa opened hers. Together the two children whispered:

RAZ AND JESSA: Mama . . .

Scene 57

"That Is How the Three Wisest Men Sat on the Banks of the Potomac."

Decatur Bronson, Raz/Chorus,
Chester Manton Saunders/Chorus and Company

CHORUS 2: And at that same moment . . . Bronson looked down at Raz and saw . . .

BRONSON: A child . . . Lord! I'm a Christian man! And it's Christmas Eve! Open your eyes. And give me your hand. I'm inviting you to supper. Because if you are my guest, then you can't be my prisoner. And I won't have to break my vow.

RAZ: What?!

BRONSON: You are welcome under my roof. Give me your hand and you are welcome to my supper—

RAZ/CHORUS: And whether it was the sound of his stomach growling, or the call of his better angel, Raz Franklin gladly shook the hand of his enemy, his host—

CHESTER/CHORUS: And Chester Manton Saunders, who could not shoot a man, but could serve him supper, came racing to the smithy with two plump chickens on a spit.

RAZ: Never again would Christmas dinner taste so sweet!

CHESTER: Decatur Bronson made a Christmas vow.

BRONSON: Next Christmas, Rose and I will toast each other.

CHESTER: To you and your wife.

BRONSON: To Rose!

BRONSON, RAZ AND CHESTER: To Rose!

CHORUS 2: And that is how the three wisest men in the country drank yuletide toasts on the banks of the Potomac.

Scene 58

AT THE WHITE HOUSE: "MRS. LINCOLN PREPARED THE PRESIDENT FOR HIS SURPRISE."

*Mary Todd Lincoln, Abraham Lincoln,
Sergeant-at-Arms and Chorus*

At the White House, Mrs. Lincoln tiptoes and puts her hands over Lincoln's eyes.

MARY TODD LINCOLN: Now, Father, close your eyes . . .

CHORUS 1: And meanwhile, back at the White House, Mrs. Lincoln prepared the president for his surprise . . .

(A nervous Sergeant-at-Arms stands at the Blue Room door.)

MARY TODD LINCOLN: Are they closed?

LINCOLN: Whatever can it be?

(Mrs. Lincoln sings: "Ta-da!" She gestures grandly to a now vacant spot onstage.)

MARY TODD LINCOLN: What . . . where is the Christmas tree? Sergeant, where is the tree?

(The terrified Sergeant-at-Arms looks significantly at President Lincoln.)

SERGEANT-AT-ARMS: I don't know what tree you are referring to, ma'am. I haven't seen any tree.

(All the fear of madness seizes Mary Todd Lincoln.)

MARY TODD LINCOLN: Father . . . Father . . . there was a tree, it was to be a surprise, a large Christmas tree . . . I am losing my mind, oh God, losing my mind on Christmas!

LINCOLN: Mother, calm yourself. Calm. I'm sure it was here. It's just gone now. This is the White House. It's a very big house. And things . . . disappear.

MARY TODD LINCOLN: But it was to be your Christmas gift, Father!

LINCOLN: I'm happy if you are, Mother . . . and I do have a gift for you. I'll bet you thought I'd forgotten, eh, with my muddled mind . . . but . . . Ta-da!

(Lincoln gives Mrs. Lincoln a box. She unwraps it.)

CHORUS 1: And so Mary Todd Lincoln got a pair of gloves, exactly like the other three hundred pair she had worn once and tossed away.

MARY TODD LINCOLN: I will treasure them always.

(The Lincolns hug.)

Scene 59

AT THE HOME FOR DESTITUTE WOMEN AND CHILDREN:
"MRS. KECKLEY GAVE HANNAH
THE BEST CHRISTMAS PRESENT EVER . . ."

Hannah/Chorus, Jessa, Mrs. Keckley/Chorus and Walker Lewis

Walker, carrying Jessa, and Mrs. Keckley reach the home, where Hannah waits.

HANNAH/CHORUS: And Jessa's mother heard the carriage coming, and was out on that porch in the cold, hungering for her child.

JESSA: Mama!

KECKLEY/CHORUS: With the help of her friend Walker Lewis, Mrs. Keckley gave Hannah the best Christmas present ever . . .

Scene 60

IN THE WHITE HOUSE:
"THEY HAD THE HOPE OF PEACE."

Abraham Lincoln/Chorus and Mary Todd Lincoln

LINCOLN/CHORUS: And as the Lincolns shared a toast on Christmas Eve, they gave each other the gladness of their hearts.

MARY TODD LINCOLN/CHORUS: And the Lincolns had what was perhaps their happiest Christmas together in a very long time. For they had the hope of Peace, which may be sweeter than peace itself.

Scene 61

CHRISTMAS MORNING: "MOSES HAD LEFT HIS BODY BEHIND HIM . . ."

Moses Levy/Chorus

MOSES/CHORUS: And on Christmas morning, Moses had left his body behind him, cast off like old clothes. And his spirit found itself back in New York; he was on the Bowery, striding down the Lower East Side—and he began to run towards Orchard Street!

Scene 62

FINALE: "ALL OVER WASHINGTON, WE CELEBRATED CHRISTMAS."

Mrs. Keckley, Mary Todd Lincoln, Jessa, Chester Manton Saunders, Decatur Bronson and Company

KECKLEY: A bit more to the right! A bit more!

(Lights up on the full Company positioning a beautiful evergreen in the parlor of the Cox Home. Walker carries Jessa on his shoulders.)

WALKER/CHORUS: And as the youngest arrival in the Cox Home:
JESSA: I got to put the star on the tree!

ALL *(Singing)*:
> O, Christmas tree! O, Christmas tree!
> Thy leaves are so unchanging.
> Not only green when summer's here,
> But also when tis cold and drear.
> O, Christmas tree! O, Christmas tree!
> Thy leaves are so unchanging . . .

KECKLEY/CHORUS: Yet in the midst of all the revelry that night, there was a sudden hush that could be heard:

MARY TODD LINCOLN/CHORUS: In the White House—

CHORUS 1: In the home—

CHESTER/CHORUS: On the river—

LONGFELLOW/CHORUS: In a poet's study all the way up in Massachusetts!

BRONSON/CHORUS: And in that hush, we bowed our heads and prayed.

KECKLEY/CHORUS: That there would be armies to search for every child . . .

RAZ/CHORUS: Regiments with hammers to rebuild the roofs . . .

ROSE/CHORUS: And with our hands,

BRONSON/CHORUS: Our own two hands we shall beat swords into plowshares.

(The bells strike midnight.)

ALL:

> I heard the bells on Christmas Day
> Their old familiar carols play
> And wild and sweet
> The words repeat
> Of peace on Earth, goodwill to men!
> Then, ringing, singing on its way,
> The world revolved from night to day,
> A voice, a chime, a chant sublime,
> Of peace on Earth, goodwill to men.

KECKLEY/CHORUS: And so our stories end.

BRONSON/CHORUS: We share with you the gladness of our hearts, and our wishes for peace. Good night.

END OF PLAY

Afterword

A Conversation with
Doris Kearns Goodwin
and Paula Vogel

————◈————

Moderated by Charles Haugland,
Huntington Theatre Company, Boston, December 2009

DKG: An interesting part for me in watching *A Civil War Christmas* was the character of Mary. She is also (obviously) . . . a character in my book [*Team of Rivals: The Political Genius of Abraham Lincoln,* 2005]. She was probably a manic-depressive. From the time she was a little girl they said she would be in either the attic or the cellar, and she had many sadnesses in her life. It takes me about a hundred pages to tell Mary's story, yet you capture her in that one scene when she is trimming the tree. You were able to create the many moods she had. You saw the sadness, you saw the manic side, even her shaking, as she was trimming the tree, and all those other parts of her: the loss of Willie, the love for Lincoln, the insecurities that she had. You captured them all, and I am in awe of something like that, what you as a dramatist were able to do.

123

PV: Thank you. This was the longest amount of time I've ever spent to research anything, and it became so addictive. I gave myself a period of about ten years, and I realized that the next step, if I didn't stop reading (the last two books I read were *Team of Rivals* and *This Republic of Suffering* [by Drew Gilpin Faust, 2008]), was that I would become a reenactor—

DKG: We could go around together!

PV: What an amazing incredible field of richness! And I'm so glad I read *Team of Rivals*! An earlier script of mine had Attorney General Bates in it. And I said: "Oops!"

DKG: He'd been gone by then.

PV: But I remember talking to Jean Baker (writer of the book *Mary Todd Lincoln*). As historians you spend so much of your life really reading those letters—and I wanted to be respectful. I hadn't started writing yet—and she said: "I have just one thing to ask you, young lady. Do not make her crazy. She was not crazy."

Now that's difficult. I wrote that scene that's gaslighting her, but people were basically treating her that way. *Every* character is so complex. That is the problem when you are trying to write a Christmas play, a holiday play or a pageant: time is limited, so you can only get one or two facets. She's a much more complex woman—the one you presented in *Team of Rivals*, than I could ever hope to do. At one point friends were telling me: "You know, people have to get home to their holiday suppers . . . you have to start taking out some of the stories, some of the plots, and one of the places I did have to cut was Mary Todd Lincoln. In an earlier version, during the Christmas tree scene, I tell how there had been an assassination plot earlier on at the soldiers home. She liked to take her husband out as often as she could for carriage rides. And someone had removed the carriage pins. He was supposed to be on that carriage ride but wasn't.

DKG: But she was, and she was hurt badly.

PV: She dashed her head on the pavement and almost died—and every time I hear about her erratic behavior in her last couple of years I have to think that there was neurological damage.

DKG: And not only that, it's interesting you mention Jean Baker, because I think those of us who are women historians feel that the men haven't given her a fair chance. There's been huge arguments in the Lincoln community about it. We know what happened to Mary at the end of her life. She was committed to an insane asylum by her son Robert because she was out on the streets, sometimes just running around without a lot of clothes on. She actually got herself out within months of being there by talking her way out with a woman lawyer. Sadly, she went back to live in the mansion on the hill in Springfield where she first met Lincoln.

When you think of what happened in her life: first of all her mother died when she was six or seven years old; her father, then married again, and the stepmother was very unkind to all the kids who were Mary's part of the family; then, eventually she falls in love with Lincoln (and I can understand why he fell in love with her—she loved Shakespeare, she loved drama, she loved poetry, she loved politics, something very few women did at that time). And all those years when he was not succeeding in politics, she believed in his destiny. But then she loses one child, Edward, who was three years old, and loss was very difficult for her. (That is one of the themes of this play: everybody is coming to terms with loss and the renewal almost at the same time.)

She gets into the White House. But, because her father and her family were Confederates (she had four half-brothers in the Confederate army, several of whom died), the people in the North never fully trusted her. The women in the East never trusted her because she came from the frontier. So she tried to make her mark by renovating the White House, as you mention in the play, but she overspent the appropriations—when the soldiers didn't have blankets—and it made Lincoln upset.

And then she loses Willie, and Willie was the one most like Lincoln: he wrote poetry, even at age ten, and he was sensitive and kind to his little brother Tad, who had a speech defect. No one outside the family could understand what he was saying. When Willie died she became somewhat unhinged. Another interesting thing you bring up in the play, is that for months she is hardly ever getting out of her bed, and Lincoln has to become mother and father for that youngest child, Tad, who is only eight years old. But then she starts going to the hospitals. Somehow she is strong when she's there; she sees everyone else's loss and the need to cope—she's beginning to come back to herself again.

The really sad thing is that on the last day of Lincoln's life, which you capture here by the "gladness of the heart" (because you end the play on Christmas Day rather than on the calendar day of Lincoln's life), it's very true that it was Lincoln's happiest day, because he knew the war was coming to an end. He asked Mary to go on a carriage ride with him that afternoon, and the theatre would be that night—where he would be killed. She was so excited that he was taking *her* on a carriage ride that day and he said, "Mary, we've been sad for so long, because of Willie's death, because of the war. The war is now coming to an end, time is healing us, we have to try and be happy again." And they talked about where they might want to go when the presidency was over: she wanted to go to Europe, he wanted to go to the Holy Land, they both wanted to go to California. There is such sadness somehow to think that that night ended what might have been a reconciliation and a strengthening for Mary. Then, of course, she loses her husband, and then Tad dies at eighteen— little wonder that this woman becomes unhinged at the end of her life.

PV: Right. You know, this is kind of terrible to say to a historian who has done all of this research, but because we do know of all of the pain and all of the suffering, I thought of two things when I wanted to write this play: I remembered watching the movie *Boys Don't Cry*, and knowing what a horrible ending there was to that story, but how wonderful it was that the filmmaker gave the last evening of peace and joy and acceptance. So I thought I would put that carriage ride on the last day, on Christmas.

But the other guiding principle, which may sound somewhat facetious, but I don't mean it to be, is I drew from my favorite cartoon, which appeared in the *New Yorker* many years ago, by the cartoonist Roz Chast. In it she had graphed two lifelines: one was the lifeline of Kafka and the other one was Daniel Boone. These two lifelines crossed in the middle. So, Kafka: age five, first nervous breakdown; writes *The Castle*; fiancée rejects him; commits suicide. Then Daniel Boone: wrestled his first alligator; elected to Congress; dies at the Alamo! And in the middle she'd drawn these two intersecting lines, with a little circle, and in the middle it said: "Liked to eat raw dough." When I saw that, I thought, that's it! I've got to find the raw dough!

DKG: Wow. Fascinating.

PV: On December 24, 1864.

I had also been thinking about the holidays—to me they are so much about mothers and children. Then I thought about Mary Surratt and Mary Todd Lincoln having the same name, and also the Virgin Mary. I thought, where is the raw dough? Well, they've got to be looking for the Christmas tree.

You try to find how collisions happen. And of course it seems coincidental, but when I read histories such as yours, I find so much coincidence, say, between Seward (secretary of state) and Bates.

DKG: It's so interesting you are saying that, because one of the ways I do my research is by creating huge chronologies of all my characters (I haven't thought about it as "where's the raw dough") because there's certain ways they intersect, or there's certain times of their life where something's happening to one that's not happening to the other that influences it the other's life. This is a difference between the way I write and what you're able to do: You can play with chronology in a certain way—in your play things went back and forward—on a stage, that's easier to do than it is with other writing, I think. So it gives you a freedom. The other great freedom, of course—I always ask my husband the difference between writing *Two Men of Florence* for characters he created versus my writing for presidents Lyndon Johnson, John F. Kennedy or Bobby Kennedy, and he said— "You can make your characters say whatever you want them to, they're yours!" I can only go to a certain level in the writing of history, I know what my characters might be thinking, but if I haven't got evidence of that by somebody having written it down in a letter, then I can't use it. You can say, "He must have done that," but that's difficult. *You* can make up people, which is fun!

PV: This is like a conversation I had with my dearly departed mother-in-law, who wrote histories for young adults—Dorothy Sterling. I used her library to start some of the reading and it was the same: "Well, how do you know what they're saying?" Or, "How can you say that?" There's a reason why we often use dramatic license, and hope it gets us through.

CH: One of my favorite moments in the play is Lincoln's ride at night where he composes his second inaugural about "let us bind up the wounds" of the country. Perhaps you could talk about whether you still think we're in the work of that second inaugural. Paula, you've talked about the wounds of our country now, the wounds of polarization—do you see those as being related?

DKG: To go backward for a moment, what struck me as so interesting about the play is that in some ways the theme of the second inaugural, even though Lincoln has a real tough voice when he talks about what God is going to do (maybe to pay back for all those years that the slaves have been in bondage), is that theme of reconciliation: "with malice towards none, with charity for all." That's a theme that's strung throughout the play, for example, with that guy finally not shooting Molly [Schreiber who plays Raz]. Even after Fort Pillow, when that massacre of the African-American troops took place, there was a question: Should the North retaliate when they found Confederates to be that way. Every part of Lincoln warred against that, even though there was such a desire to retaliate against the Confederates. And forgiveness is part of the second inaugural, forgiveness is part of the retaliation theme in the play—forgiveness—it's all connected in together.

PV: Right. I wrote this at what was for me a time of mourning—2006. Even though I'd had the idea and started the reading in 1997, it was post-Katrina when I wrote this. I was in mourning, thinking we may lose our country and who we are.

I recognize that you have written about such a large period of time, and I'd like to think that there's a belief that historians have of a pendulum, of a forward movement: two steps back, but one step further forward. As a dramatist I'm afraid I think at times: Is the catastrophe coming? So, in 2006, writing this post-Katrina, writing this as the immigration debate became yet another "value" causing us to fractionalize, sections of our country still talking about states rights, I thought, We still have not addressed race, we are still using wedges to divide the political electorate—I did write this in a state of mourning.

What is interesting to me in this second production, because the first was done last year [2008], right after the election, (and I am so grateful to the Huntington and Peter [DuBois] for giving me this period to go back in; and for the company to look at it and do some rewrites; and for people who say, "Oh by the way, Bates had resigned in 1864," and all of that good stuff) is that

I'm thinking about: Where are we right now? What's happening right now in terms of health care? What about our anxiety level? In terms of this president—where people have managed to get past the guards and crash a White House party—makes me feel very different.

DKG: Yes, that's another theme in the play: when you talked about the fact that anybody could come into the White House—that's absolutely true in those days. In fact, Lincoln would often face the morning with two hours of talking to ordinary people who would come just to tell him they needed a job—these were the days before the Secret Service, so if you wanted to come and see the president you could just line up and go sit in front of the Oval Office and go and talk to him. And after a while his secretaries, Nicolay and Hay, would say to him: "Lincoln, you don't have time for these ordinary people." He said: "You're wrong—these are my public-opinion baths; I must never forget the popular assembly from which I have come." And then he would have these huge public receptions; anybody could come. So those "stupid people" who then ended up going into the White House would actually be welcome! Backwoodsmen would be standing side by side with diplomats and Lincoln would shake every hand. There's a great story connected to that: he finally was going to sign the Emancipation Proclamation on January 1, 1863, but that morning at a New Year's reception he had shaken so many hands—thousands of hands—that when he went to sign the Emancipation Proclamation his hand was numb and shaking, so he put the pen down. He said: "If ever my soul were in an act, it is in this act, but if I sign with a shaking hand, posterity will say, he hesitated." So he waited and waited until he could take up the pen and sign with a bold and clear hand.

AUDIENCE MEMBER: Have you considered what Lincoln's place would have been had he lived?

130

DKG: Lincoln said in those last months before he died that he knew the act of bringing back the South into the Union and reconstructing the country was probably the most challenging act ever facing any statesman, even more than the war itself. So had he lived there's no question that it would have still been messy, probably, and maybe his reputation—dying just at that moment so we could imagine how much better it would have been—might have been to some extent sullied on the other hand. He was the best friend that the South could ever have wanted. And given his desire to somehow bring them back without losing the benefits that black Americans had been given, the genius who had won the war, the man who would have had the authority of winning that war behind him, you just have to hope that things would have been better. Even if it would have made him a more complex character.

I think that that was one of the hardest things for me: I couldn't have a happy ending to my book because he died at the end. But I couldn't bear to end it there, after having lived with him for ten years. So it was thrilling when I finally found one way to end my book that could make me happy. Lincoln had always wanted more than anything to be remembered *after* he died. He felt people live on in the memory of others, especially if they've accomplished something that's worthy. (In fact that's what's also so interesting also about Willie's death; he talked about Willie all the time to keep him alive.) So his dream was to do something worthy enough to be remembered after he died.

I was able to find this incredible interview with Leo Tolstoy that he gave to a New York newspaper in 1908, in which he talked about having recently gone to a very remote area of the Caucasus (perhaps like Chechnya today), where there were a group of wild barbarians who had never left that part of Russia. When they knew Tolstoy was in their mix, they were so excited! They said: "Tell us stories about the Great Men of History." So, he said: "I told them about Napoleon and Alexander the Great and Frederick the Great, but before I finished the chief of the barbarians stood up and said: 'But wait you haven't told us about that greatest ruler of them all! We want to hear about that man who spoke with the voice of thunder, who laughed like the sunrise, who came from that place called America that is so far from here that if a young man should travel there he would be an old man when he arrived. Tell us of that man, tell us of Abraham Lincoln.'" And Tolstoy said he was stunned to know that Lincoln's name had reached this far. He told them everything he could. And then he told them, and this is what made Lincoln so great, he said: "Hc wasn't as great a general as Napoleon and not as great a statesman as Frederick the Great—his greatness consisted in the integrity of his character and the moral fiber of his being." As soon as I found that, that was the ending of my book. I could make it happy in the end.

PV: That's great. It's an interesting thing: thinking about memory. Another profound experience in my life is that I've been lucky to spend a lot of time in Alaska, which is one of the most beautiful spots on earth. And there is one of the most spiritual places I've ever been: it's a totem monument museum on Sitka Island, with these unbelievably beautiful totem poles. Then, in the midst of tall pines, you turn the corner, and there you see at the top of this one totem pole Abraham Lincoln in his stove pipe hat. It is an extraordinary site—the reach of his memory.

DKG: Wow.

PV: It's interesting that as historians, in essence, you keep memory alive. I wrestled a lot with how to end the play, because I wanted a kind of forward movement. The original ending actually dealt with what happened to Bronson (Bronson is a combination of two real-life Medal of Honor winners) and his wife, and Chester and Raz in adulthood. I wanted a kind of flash-forward, so we would experience the memory of reconciliation that was to come.

DKG: But you did get it. After not killing the little boy, Bronson says, "I will see Rose next Christmas . . ."

PV: I'm sad about all the back stories I had to weave out. I had to cut a story about Rose and Bronson traveling to San Francisco—deciding to go neither North or South, they head West.

DKG: Wow.

PV: And having ten children crowding around the table.

DKG: I know, sometimes people ask me: "Why didn't you say more about Vice President Hannibal Hamlin?" I keep saying: "This book is so fat now you need a roller at the airport to carry it around—no way!"

PV: I'd like to hear more about Vice President Hamlin, actually!

DKG: I think your question before raises a big historical question: Did the man make the times or the times make the man? Lincoln himself understood that sometimes you need huge challenges for somebody to be well recognized. When he was a young man he gave a speech in which he worried that his entire generation didn't have challenges as great as the founding fathers, that there was nothing left for his generation but material ambitions. But then, of course, he gets this huge challenge: the country splitting apart in the fifties. His real worry was not simply the North and the South splitting each other apart, but that if they did that then some day the West would cut off from the East. Then the whole idea of what America stood for—that ordinary people could govern themselves, that you really didn't have to be an aristocracy or a monarchy or a dictatorship—would be undone. That's what the founding fathers had created, which made us a beacon of hope for everybody. So you're right: that huge challenge he faced and then meeting it allowed him to become the man that we so revere.

AUDIENCE MEMBER: Has writing one play that deals with history whet your appetite?

PV: Absolutely. I'm a little worried about the amount of time I have left on this earth . . . um . . . But, actually, I have become interested in World War II, specifically the war in the Pacific theater. —You know, I don't actually think about them as historical plays—once I see a moment I can't stop thinking about it. I have started reading World War II history. But, music for me is living history. So I've been listening to all of the wonderful songs that I heard growing up, the songs that my mother danced to. That and the officers' clubs in Washington, D.C., have made the subject not feel like history to me.

It's so hard right now with the economy to mount a play this size. Blessedly, we manage to get talented children and graduate students to put this on. As American artists we should be looking back, but it's an expensive proposition—particularly for women playwrights. I just had a friend say: We'd love to do a new play of yours. And I said: "Okay, if I can sit down and do a play with two characters, two stools and a spotlight—knowing your budget— it's yours!"

We have so many talented writers in this town—just on the Civil War alone. Here's a story I'd love to see one of them take on as a drama: early in the war, there was a little hiatus in battle when there was actually a baseball game between Union soldiers and Confederates. Will someone please write that play?

AUDIENCE MEMBER: Were there a lot of differences, rewrites, between the first production and the second?

PV: So many things changed! I was really fortunate to have worked with historians who read drafts in Washington, D.C.

I also worked with historians in African-American military history. There were so many things, like—it broke my heart—I had General Daniel Sickles as a character—

DKG: Oh, he's a big character!

PV: He's so fun!—I'm hoping someone does the musical-theatre evening with General Daniel Sickles . . .

DKG: He actually killed somebody—

PV: and Edwin Stanton—

DKG: —secretary of war—

PV: —was his lawyer! First insanity-defense plea.

DKG: His wife was having an affair with Francis Scott Key's son, Philip Barton Key. Daniel Sickles killed him in broad daylight. Then Stanton, who later becomes part of the Cabinet, becomes his lawyer and gets him off on temporary insanity. Then Sickles goes into the war, loses his leg at Gettysburg, and becomes a hero. He was a congressman at the time.

PV: He's a fascinating character. After his leg was amputated, he used to visit his leg—and bring flowers! You can't make this stuff up. And he was a real Romeo. One of the things I had to cut was him on crutches, chasing married women through the streets. These women would run—very slowly—so that he could catch up with them! There are many things like that I had to cut. There is a great book, *American Scoundrel*, that details all this.

DKG: Linking all of those different groups of people together is one of the best parts of the play. That's also a whole new genre in history writing. And a lot of it is being written by women historians. They are not just looking at the characters that I tend to deal with—these guys, the presidents— (unfortunately if you're writing about presidents, you are writing about men), but factoring in the immigrant groups that have come, understanding the African-American experience, understanding the women's experience, and that whole level of society generally considered to be below the people on the top.

PV: It is a wonderful time to be a reader, because so much is coming forward. I was reading terrific stuff like *The Battle for Christmas*— it's a history of Christmas that I never knew. And I had built the play with songs, and thought, I had better find something to back me up, like Clara Barton (I'm sure she was not in Washington, D.C., but there's no record that she wasn't . . .). I had Whitman in the play, then found that he'd taken ill. I thought, How do I work my way out of that? I had wanted to include "The Yellow Rose of Texas" with "Lo, How a Rose," yet I couldn't find the historical evidence. Then I found this book of essays in which someone wrote about abductions of civilians after Gettysburg— this was very near the spot I'd wanted to choose for the supply depot. I was lucky.

AUDIENCE MEMBER: What are the challenges of portraying characters from earlier, historic periods?

PV: I'm not a historian; my brother was the kind of amateur historian in the family. He died of AIDS in 1988, and I was his caretaker. He said I want you to teach the children our family history, they have to know where we came from. And I didn't know how to do that and it took me a long time to figure out how to do it. I wrote this play as a very sentimental aunt and godmother. I wrote this play for every ancestor who sits around my table who celebrates Christmas but also has lit the lights on Hanukkah, I'm writing this for my family who celebrates Kwanzaa. So, I just wanted to fulfill that promise to my brother

Carl. I'm not a historian, but what I'm hoping is that when the kids in my family walk on the streets of Washington, they will think of that place as their legacy. These stories are *our* stories of American history. I wanted to give a gift back. It took my a very long time, but I'm very lucky to be living at a time when we do have women historians, when we do have African-American historians, when we do have people who are helping us *remember* so we as a country right now, faced with enormous challenges, can talk to each other and hopefully get in a civic dialogue. That's what I want to give my kids. I started crying when the concept came into my head, but I just wanted to tell a story.

DKG: And so you have—you've told a great story. And what a perfect way to end.

DORIS KEARNS GOODWIN is the Pulitzer Prize–winning author of many presidential histories, including *Team of Rivals: The Political Genius of Abraham Lincoln*; *No Ordinary Time: Franklin and Eleanor Roosevelt: The Home Front in World War II*; and *The Fitzgeralds and the Kennedys: An American Saga*.

CHARLES HAUGLAND manages artistic programs and dramaturgy for Huntington Theatre Company.

Further Reading

Music of the Civil War

------⋅◄◆►⋅------

$\mathcal{M}$usic was as big a part of life in 1864 as it is today, especially during the holiday season, and it is everywhere in *A Civil War Christmas*. You may be surprised to hear so many familiar songs in a play set so long ago, but many of our favorite songs were just as popular during the Civil War. The many types of music in that time period reflected the abundance of diversity in America.

CHRISTMAS CAROLS

Though many Christmas carols originated in England, Americans wrote new songs as they developed their own traditions. Some of today's best known carols and hymns were written around the time of the Civil War, including: "It Came Upon a Midnight Clear" (1849), "We Three Kings of Orient Are" (1857) and "O Little Town of Bethlehem" (1868). Here are some other Christmas carols that are sung in *A Civil War Christmas*:

"Angels We Have Heard On High": Lyrics based on the traditional French carol "Les Anges dans nos Campagnes" (literally, "The Angels in Our Countryside"). The best known English version was translated around 1860 by James Chadwick.

"Children, Go Where I Send Thee": A traditional African-American carol. The author is unknown. Also known as "The Carol of the Twelve Numbers" and "Little Bitty Baby."

"Ding Dong! Merrily on High": Translated from a French carol that dates back to the sixteenth century. English lyrics by George R. Woodward, approximately 1924.

"God Rest Ye Merry Gentlemen": Popular early carol, first published in Great Britain in 1833.

"The Holly and the Ivy": Possible pagan origins could date this song back to more than one thousand years. The music and most of the text was collected by English folklorist Cecil Sharp from a woman in Gloucestershire. This carol is probably related to an older carol "The Contest of the Ivy and the Holly," a contest between the traditional emblems of woman and man, respectively.

"I Heard the Bells on Christmas Day": Lyrics by Henry Wadsworth Longfellow, 1863. Music, "Waltham," by John B. Calkin, 1872.

"Lo, How a Rose E'er Blooming": An anonymous German carol, which first appeared in the late sixteenth century. The best known music appeared in the *Speyer Hymnal* printed in Cologne in 1599, with harmonization written by German composer Michael Praetorius in 1609.

"O Tannenbaum": A German carol set to an old folk tune. The best known version was written by Ernst Anschütz in 1824. A Tannenbaum is a fir tree (die Tanne) or Christmas tree (der Weihnachtsbaum).

"Rise Up, Shepherd, and Follow": African-American spiritual first published in the U.S. in 1867.

"Silent Night" ("Stille Nacht"): Original German lyrics by Josef Mohr in 1816; original music by Franz Xaver Gruber in 1818.

"Sister Mary Had-a But One Child" [Ain't That A'Rocking?]: Traditional African-American spiritual.

"What Child Is This?": Lyrics by William C. Dix, 1865. Set to the traditional sixteenth century English melody "Greensleeves."

MILITARY MUSIC

Just as many Christmas carols evolved out of songs from other cultures, soldiers borrowed melodies from their ancestors to sing on the battlefield. New songs were also invented to capture the mood and circumstances of each war. Here are some examples of military music used in *A Civil War Christmas*:

"All Quiet Along the Potomac Tonight": Music by Confederate soldier John Hill Hewitt; lyrics by New York poet Ethel Lynn Beers, 1863, based on her poem "The Picket Guard." Published in *Harper's Weekly* on November 30, 1861. A genuine (if unintentional) North-South collaboration, it enjoyed tremendous popularity on both sides of the lines.

"The Girl I Left Behind Me": A traditional fife tune imported from England that became especially popular during the Revolution. It was known in Ireland as "The Rambling Laborer" and first published in Dublin in 1791.

"Good Ol' Rebel Soldier": Lyrics by Confederate Major Innes Randolph; music set to the old Irish tune "Joe Bowers."

143

"The Liberty Ball" or "Lincoln and Liberty": First collected in *Hutchinson's Republican Songster* of 1860, with music set to "Rosin the Beau." The Hutchinson Family was a large family singing group from New Hampshire who popularized many Civil War tunes.

"[While We Were] Marching Through Georgia": A marching song written by Henry Clay Work in 1865, referencing Union General William T. Sherman's "March to the Sea" campaign in 1864. It was widely popular with Union Army veterans after the war. However, General Sherman himself despised the song, in part because it was played at almost every public appearance that he attended.

"Maryland, My Maryland": Lyrics by James Ryder Randall, set to the music of the Christmas carol "O Tannenbaum." On April 19, 1861, soldiers of the 6th Massachusetts Infantry were attacked by a pro-secession mob as they passed through Baltimore, Maryland, on their way to Washington, D.C. Although the lyrics suggest that Maryland was on the verge of joining the Confederacy, the state remained loyal to the Union. In 1939, the state's general assembly adopted "Maryland, My Maryland" as the state song.

"Secesh" [Shiloh]: John Hartford, a fiddler, was taught this song by Howdy Forrester. In middle Tennessee the Secessionists were known as the "Secesh." It was considered a brave act for men to enlist when thousands of soldiers were killed in a single battle, as happened in Shiloh.

OTHER SONGS

"Follow the Drinking Gourd": This song was supposedly used by the Underground Railroad. The song contained a secret map that led fleeing slaves North. Simply, the "drinking gourd" refers to a hollow gourd used by slaves as a water dipper. The song uses the term in order to refer to the Big Dipper, which points North. H. B. Parks "found" the song, and it was published in 1928 by the Texas Folklore Society. A popular revival of the song occurred during the civil rights and folk music movements of the 1950s and 1960s.

"I Wonder as I Wander": John Jacob Niles based the song on music he heard in Murphy, North Carolina, in 1933, after hearing a girl named Annie Morgan sing a fascinating tune. From three lines of verse, he developed the rest of the melody himself.

"The Yellow Rose of Texas": A traditional folk song, considered the unofficial state song of Texas. The actual author is unknown. The original publisher (Firth, Pond & Co.) only stated that it was composed and arranged expressly for Charles H. Brown by "J. K." The A. Henry Moss Papers in the Center for American History contain an unpublished early handwritten version of what may be a similar song, perhaps dating from the time of the Battle of San Jacinto in 1836. (The soundtrack to the TV miniseries *James A. Michener's Texas* dates the song to 1927 and co-credits its authorship to Gene Autry and Jimmy Long.)

Compiled by Noëlle G-M Gibbs for Long Wharf Theatre, as accompanying material for its production of A Civil War Christmas. *Ms. Gibbs worked on the world premiere of* A Civil War Christmas *as a research assistant and on the west coast premiere of the production as the assistant director.*

She holds BAs in Theater and Dance from UC San Diego, and is a graduate of the Accademia dell'Arte in Arezzo, Italy. She is a director, teaching artist, dramaturg and performer who has worked as an assistant director at Shakespeare Santa Cruz, Long Wharf Theatre, TheatreWorks of Silicon Valley and Magic Theatre. Currently, she is the Associate Artistic Director of Portola Valley Theatre Conservatory, where she manages an afterschool-theater program for students in pre-K through high school, and directs musicals and dramatic works.

Singing Soldiers:

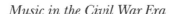

Music in the Civil War Era

Tonight, as I was trying to keep cool, sitting by a wounded soldier in Armory Square, I was attracted by some pleasant singing in an adjoining ward . . . The principal singer was a young lady-nurse of one of the wards, accompanying on a melodeon, and join'd by the lady-nurses of other wards. They sat there, making a charming group, with their handsome, healthy faces, and standing up a little behind them were some ten or fifteen of the convalescent soldiers, young men, nurses, etc., with books in their hands, singing.

—*Walt Whitman*, Specimen Days

*W*hen soldiers went to the battlefront in the 1860s, they brought a startling number of instruments: banjos, fiddles, tin whistles, mandolins and guitars. As Civil War historian Bell Irvin Wiley writes: "The men who wore the blue, and the butternut Rebs who opposed them, more than American fighters of any period, deserve to be called singing soldiers." (*The Life of*

Billy Yank, Louisiana State University Press, 1952, 1978.) At the front, soldiers learned many new songs to supplement the traditional hymns, drinking songs and Christmas carols they had known at home.

Songs written in the Civil War era often told the stories of major battles and historic events with newspaper-like immediacy. When Major General Sherman gave Savannah to President Lincoln as a Christmas gift, songwriter Henry Clay Work commemorated the campaign within months with "[While We Were] Marching Through Georgia." Ballads like "Dixie" and "The Liberty Ball" spread ideology and fed nationalism on both sides. Drums created the rhythm of battle and the beat for a march; most units had an infantry band, leading General Robert E. Lee to claim: "You cannot have an army without music."

African-American spirituals also became a widespread musical tradition during the Civil War and the years that followed. As newly freed or fugitive men and women made their way North, they carried with them songs they had learned orally on plantations. "Follow the Drinking Gourd" is believed to have begun as a way to memorize the map of the Underground Railroad. While the history of many songs from the era is well documented, the original authors of many spirituals like "Children, Go Where I Send Thee" and "Rise Up, Shepherd, and Follow" remain unknown.

Soldiers and civilians alike greeted Christmas reluctantly during the war, reminded of the conflict's bleak insanity. Henry Wadsworth Longfellow captured the sentiment, writing how "The cannon thundered in the South / And with the sound / The carols drowned / Of peace on earth, goodwill to men."

But historian James McIvor shares a brighter anecdote in his book *God Rest Ye Merry, Soldiers* (Viking, 2005): on Christmas Eve, 1862, in Tennessee, Union and Confederate troops camped in close proximity, near enough to hear each other's bands. At first, they played nationalist songs back and forth, but when the Union army played the ballad "Home, Sweet Home," the Confederates joined with them. All the men could hear the other camp sing, and there was no attack that night. One of those soldiers, Samuel Seay, wrote: "And, after our bands had ceased playing, we could hear the sweet refrain as it died away on the cool frosty air."

Written by Charles Haugland, Huntington Theatre Company, as accompanying material for its production of A Civil War Christmas.

Testimonies of the Faithful

——•:❖:•——

We must have the faith that things will work out somehow, that God will make a way for us when there seems
no way.

—*Martin Luther King, Jr.*

*S*oldiers, officers and chaplains often improvised around
the holidays to re-create traditions and remember loved
ones. They did their best to organize Christmas or Passover cele-
brations. "'Holiday season charity was not forgotten this year,'"
wrote one Michigan soldier. On Christmas Day 1864, ninety Michigan men and their captain loaded up wagons with food and
supplies and distributed them to destitute civilians in the Georgia
countryside. The Union 'Santa Clauses' tied tree branches to the
heads of the mule teams to resemble reindeer." (Kevin Rawlings,
We Were Marching on Christmas Day, Toomey Press, 1997.)

While lying there, our camp duties were not of an arduous character, and being apprised of the approaching Feast of Passover, twenty of my comrades and co-religionists belonging to the regiment, united in a request to our commanding officer for relief from duty, in order that we might keep the holy days, which he readily acceded to . . . and, as the Paymaster had lately visited the regiment, he had left us plenty of greenbacks.

Our next business was to find some suitable person to proceed to Cincinnati, Ohio, to buy us matzos . . . a supply train arrived in camp, and to our delight seven barrels of matzos. On opening them, we were surprised and pleased to find that our thoughtful sutler had enclosed two Hagedahs and prayer-books . . . We obtained two kegs of cider, a lamb, several chickens and some eggs. Horesradish or parsley we could not obtain, but in lieu we found a weed . . .

We had the lamb, but did not know what part was to represent it at the table; but Yankee ingenuity prevailed, and it was decided to cook the whole and put it on the table, then we could dine off it, and be sure we had the right part. The necessaries for the charoset we could not obtain, so we got a brick which, rather hard to digest, reminded us, by looking at it, for what purpose it was intended.

At dark we had all prepared, and were ready to commence the service. There being no rabbi present, I was selected to read the services, which I commenced by asking the blessing of the Almighty on the food before us, and to preserve our lives from danger . . .

There, in the wild woods of West Virginia, away from home and friends, we consecrated and offered up to the ever-loving God of Israel our prayers and sacrifice. I doubt whether the spirits of our forefathers, had they been looking down on us, standing there with our arms by our side ready for an attack, faithful to our God and our cause, would have imagined themselves amongst

152

mortals, enacting this commemoration of the scene that transpired in Egypt.

—*J. A. Joel, from a Union camp in 1861, published in 1866*

We see similar scenes in *A Civil War Christmas*, when "real" coffee becomes a Christmas treat, or when a Christmas tree is the most special gift that a matron can give her children or a wife can give her husband.

In the face of destruction, the little remembrances of holiday traditions are enough to remind the faithful of the trials and tribulations of those who came before them. Small actions allow all to remember that love, peace and family are precious treasures, not to be taken for granted.

In an unexpected way, the difficulty of war allowed many people to understand the holiday season from a new perspective: one in which humility and thanksgiving became essential, making the time of year a particularly crucial component of American identity. As noted historian James McIvor said: "The Civil War made Christmas a truly American holiday in a way it had never entirely been before." (*God Rest Ye Merry, Soldiers*, Viking, 2005.)

ADJUSTING EXPECTATIONS

Remaining upbeat around the holidays became increasingly difficult, both on the field and at home, as supplies became sparse and the death toll rose:

This day, one year ago, how many thousand families, gay and joyous, celebrating Merry Christmas, drinking health to absent members of their family, and sending upon the wings of love and affection long, deep, and sincere wishes for their safe return to the loving ones at home, but today are clad in the deepest mourning in memory to some lost and loved member of their circle.

—Tally Simpson, in a letter to his sister
from Fredericksburg, Virginia, 1862

Santa Claus may not make it through the blockade to deliver presents this year . . .

—A common lamentation of Southern parents in 1862

We had many a drunken fight and knockdown before the day closed.

—A soldier in the 20th Tennessee,
after officers provided the soldiers with a barrel of whiskey
to celebrate the night, 1862

The men gathered about the campfires during the evening hours with abortive attempts at merriment, soon to be given up, and then to talk in whispers of friends and family and home. The bugle calls, holding out the promise that balmy sleep might bring forgetfulness, were welcomed; although tattoo seemed a wail, and lights-out a sob.

—Colonel Charles Manderson,
19th Ohio Infantry, 1862

The one worn-out railroad running to the far South could not bring us half enough necessary supplies, and even if it could have transported Christmas boxes of good things, the people at home were too depleted to send them.

—Confederate General Gordon,
writing from headquarters near Petersburg,
Virginia, 1864

FAITH IN THE FACE OF DESTRUCTION

Soldiers, politicians, preachers, doctors and families turned to faith as they struggled to cope with the destruction and grief caused by the Civil War. Letters to loved ones frequently contain a "God willing" or an "I pray to God," and references to faith and God appear in both Abraham Lincoln and Jefferson Davis's public speeches.

Often, the Church and government borrowed language from one another to instill a sense of nationalism rooted in spirituality among citizens in both Northern and Southern territories. The faithful did not lose hope:

> We'll fight for liberty
> Till de Lord shall call us home
> We'll soon be free
> Till de Lord shall call us home.
>
> —*Colonel Thomas Wentworth Higginson,*
> *a Massachusetts officer who organized freed slaves*
> *into the first black regiment, recorded in his diary*
> *on Christmas 1864 this simple, hopeful hymn*
> *that the slaves at Georgetown, South Carolina,*
> *were whipped for singing when Lincoln was elected*

. . . I believe, and I shall try to show, that all through these last years, and especially through this last year, there has been a great drawing back of all of us to resume and fully occupy realms of life, blessings and duties which ere never but half-occupied before . . . We ought to render up our thanks for the new power and completeness with which the ordinary blessings of God's natural providence have been received and realized, in consequence of the peculiar circumstances under which we have been living . . . More than fourscore years ago this nation declared itself free and independent—

the new ground of a new experiment in national, social and individual life. It needs no very wise historian to tell how very partially that bright announcement has been fulfilled. We have never half claimed our independence.

—*Reverend Phillips Brooks in his 1863*
Thanksgiving Day speech

Services were often ecumenical, and some members of the clergy sought to promote common beliefs with members of other religions. For example, Rabbi Illowy's sermon in Baltimore, January 1861, condones the National Fast Day:

. . . It is neither new moon nor Sabbath, but it is a day designated by the Chief Magistrate of the United States, for the purpose of fasting, humiliation and prayer. In compliance with his proclamation, we are assembled here to join our fellow citizens of the various denominations in keeping this day as a solemn fast; as a day devoted to religious exercise only.

—*Rabbi Illowy, National Fast Day Sermon,*
Baltimore, January 1861

Hannah, you wanted me to tell you the news in our camp and tent. The news in our tent is that we are trying to serve the Lord. We have prayer meetings in our tent twice a week, and one of us reads a chapter . . . We take turns. And we pray every night before laying down to sleep . . . I enjoy myself better here serving the Lord than I did at home.

—*James Gould, New York 144th Infantry,*
in a letter to his sister, 1862

I asked God for strength, that I might achieve,
I was made weak, that I might learn humbly to obey.
I asked him for health, that I might do great things,

I was given infirmity, that I might do better things.
I asked for riches, that I might be happy,
I was given poverty, that I might be wise.
I asked for power, that I might have the praise of men,
I was given weakness, that I might feel the need of God.
I asked for all things, that I might enjoy life,
I was given life, that I might enjoy all things.
I got nothing that I asked for—but everything I had
    hoped for.
Almost despite myself, my unspoken prayers were
    answered.
I am, among all men, most richly blessed.

—*By an unknown Confederate soldier*

Molly, this is a beautiful Sunday morning, and I expect
you are gone to church somewhere. You must not fail
to attend church as often as you can. I have not heard a
sermon in about four months . . . I never wanted to hear
preaching as bad in my life.

—*William Stilwell in a letter to his wife, 1862*

For the hope of peace is sweeter than peace itself.

—*Ely Parker, from the play*
A Civil War Christmas *by Paula Vogel*

*Compiled by Noëlle G-M Gibbs for Long Wharf Theatre as accompanying
material for its production of* A Civil War Christmas.

Through the Eyes of the Poet:

------··=:❖:=··------

Living Voices of the Civil War

Poetry comes nearer to vital truth than history.

Plato

*T*he poetry of the Civil War captures the conflicted experiences of a divided nation like no other written account can. The vitality of sound and space that a well-constructed poem evokes transports the reader directly to a specific battlefield or war-torn home, allowing even the modern reader to experience the war from a personal perspective.

These poems stand in memoriam of the thousands of would-be silent stories and common experiences of all those affected by war. Further, they connect the desolate photographs and drawings of the divided nation to the personal experiences of the soldiers, officers and their families.

Henry Wadsworth Longfellow, Clara Barton and Walt Whitman all make appearances in *A Civil War Christmas: An American Musical Celebration*. Their unique, personal perspectives on the situation deepen our understandings of the Civil War because

159

they represent several groups of people that we don't always consider in our study of history.

Barton and Whitman performed influential duties both on the field and off, volunteering their time to consol the injured and nurse the sick. Longfellow spent the early part of the 1860s in a state of great confusion as he reflected on national disunity and personal grief.

All three of these individuals left behind poems that capture the conflicting feelings of hope/despair and isolation/unity that characterize a war-torn nation. Their poems allude to disturbance of peace and stability as hundreds of thousands of soldiers struggle for a liberated nation.

Though Henry Wadsworth Longfellow sought liberation for all people, he was troubled by the Civil War's destructive influence on the country. The 1860s proved to be a particularly stressful period of time for the poet, not only because of the divided nation, but also because Longfellow suffered a series of personal tragedies during the decade.

In 1861, Longfellow lost his beloved wife, Frances "Fanny" Appleton to a fire. The following year, his oldest son, Charles, became a lieutenant in the Army of the Potomac, despite his father's reservations that he join up. In 1863, Charles was severely wounded by a bullet that passed under his shoulder blades, removing one of his spinal processes.

Longfellow diligently kept a journal through this period that reflects a deep sense of grief and torment, particularly around the holidays. On his first Christmas without Fanny, Longfellow wrote: "How inexpressibly sad are all holidays."

He was still grieving the following Christmas when he wrote: "A merry Christmas say the children, but that is no more for me." On Christmas Day 1864, Longfellow composed the seven-stanza poem "Christmas Bells" to reflect the mixture of grief over his family, the state of the country and the importance of God in his life:

I heard the bells on Christmas Day
Their old familiar carols play,
And wild and sweet
The words repeat
Of peace on earth, goodwill to men!

And thought how, as the day had come,
The belfries of all Christendom
Had rolled along
The unbroken song
Of peace on earth, goodwill to men!

Till, ringing, singing on its way,
The world revolved from night to day,
A voice, a chime
A chant sublime
Of peace on earth, goodwill to men!

Then from each black accursed mouth
The cannon thundered in the South,
And with the sound
The carols drowned
Of peace on earth, goodwill to men!

It was as if an earthquake rent
The hearth-stones of a continent,
And made forlorn
The households born
Of peace on earth, goodwill to men!

And in despair I bowed my head;
"There is no peace on earth," I said;
"For hate is strong,
And mocks the song
Of peace on earth, goodwill to men!"

161

Then pealed the bells more loud and deep:
"God is not dead; nor doth He sleep!
The Wrong shall fail,
The Right prevail,
With peace on earth, goodwill to men!"

This poem later provided the lyrics to the popular Christmas hymn "I Heard the Bells on Christmas Day," though the stanzas that reference the war directly are omitted in the hymn.

Clara Barton preferred to work on her own in the fields despite resistance from the government-sanctioned health organizations. She founded hospitals and care centers, brought small gifts and words of comfort to the soldiers, and proved that women could do more than sit at home and mourn during this time of conflict.

After all of her experiences (including the identification of more than twenty thousand bodies at the end of the war), Barton composed a poem in honor of all the women who helped on the front lines. Here is an excerpt from "The Women Who Went to the Field":

The women who went to the field, you say,
The *women* who went to the field; and pray,
What did they go for?—just to be in the way?—
They'd not know the difference betwixt work and play,
And what did they know about *war*, anyway?
What could they *do*?—of what *use* could they be?
They would scream at the sight of a gun, don't you see?
Just fancy them 'round where the bugle notes play,
And the long roll is bidding us on to the fray.
Imagine their skirts 'mong artillery wheels,
And watch for their flutter as they flee 'cross the fields
When the charge is rammed home and the fire belches hot;
They never will wait for the answering shot.
They would faint at the first drop of blood in their sight.

What fun for us boys— (ere we enter the fight);
They might pick some lint, and tear up some sheets,
And make us some jellies, and send on their sweets,
And knit some soft socks for Uncle Sam's shoes.
And write us some letters, and tell us the news.
And thus it was settled, by common consent,
That husbands, or brothers, or whoever went,
That the place for the women was in their own homes,
There to patiently wait until victory comes.
But later it chanced—just how no one knew—
That the lines slipped a bit, and some 'gan to crowd through;
And they went—where did they go? —Ah! where did they not?
Show us the battle—the field—or the spot
Where the groans of the wounded rang out on the air
That her ear caught it not, and her hand was not there;
Who wiped the death sweat from the cold clammy brow,
And sent home the message: "'Tis well with him now"?
Who watched in the tents whilst the fever fires burned,
And the pain-tossing limbs in agony turned,
And wet the parched tongue, calmed delirium's strife
Till the dying lips murmured, "My Mother," "My Wife"?
[. . .]
The women of question; what *did* they go for?
Because in their hearts God had planted the seed
Of pity for woe, and help for its need;
They saw, in high purpose, a duty to do,
And the armor of right broke the barriers through.
Uninvited, unaided, unsanctioned ofttimes,
With pass, or without it, they pressed on the lines;
They pressed, they implored, 'till they ran the lines through,
And that *this* was the "running" the men saw them do.
[. . .]
And what would they do if war came again?
The *scarlet cross floats* where all was blank then.
They would bind on their "*brassards*" and march to the fray,

163

And the man liveth not who could say to them nay;
They would stand with you now, as they stood with you then,
The nurses, consolers, and saviors of men.

Compiled by Noëlle G-M Gibbs for Long Wharf Theatre as accompanying material for its production of A Civil War Christmas.

Behind the Scenes:

---••§◆§••---

An Excerpt from Elizabeth Keckley's Journal

CHAPTER VII
Washington, D.C., 1862–1863

*I*n the summer of 1862, freedmen began to flock into Washington from Maryland and Virginia. They came with a great hope in their hearts, and with all their worldly goods on their backs. Fresh from the bonds of slavery, fresh from the benighted regions of the plantation, they came to the Capital looking for liberty, and many of them not knowing it when they found it. Many good friends reached forth kind hands, but the North is not warm and impulsive. For one kind word spoken, two harsh ones were uttered; there was something repelling in the atmosphere, and the bright joyous dreams of freedom to the slave faded—were sadly altered, in the presence of that stern, practical mother, reality. Instead of flowery paths, days of perpetual sunshine, and bowers hanging with golden fruit, the road was rugged and full of thorns, the sunshine was eclipsed by shadows, and the mute appeals for help too often were answered by cold neglect. Poor dusky children of slavery, men and women of my own race—the transition from slavery to freedom was too sudden for you! The bright dreams were too rudely dispelled; you were not prepared for the new life that opened before you, and the great masses of the North learned to look upon your helplessness with indifference—learned to speak of you as an idle, dependent race. Reason should have prompted kinder thoughts. Charity is ever kind.

One fair summer evening I was walking the streets of Washington, accompanied by a friend, when a band of music was heard in the distance. We wondered what it could mean, and curiosity prompted us to find out its meaning. We quickened our steps, and discovered that it came from the house of Mrs. Farnham. The yard was brilliantly lighted, ladies and gentlemen were moving about, and the band was playing some of its sweetest airs. We approached the sentinel on duty at the gate, and asked what was going on. He told us that it was a festival given for the benefit of the sick and wounded soldiers in the city. This suggested an idea to me. If the white people can give festivals to raise funds for the relief of suffering soldiers, why should not the well-to-do colored people go to work to do something for the benefit of the suffering blacks? I could not rest. The thought was ever present with me, and the next Sunday I made a suggestion in the colored church, that a society of colored people be formed to labor for the benefit of the unfortunate freedmen. The idea proved popular, and in two weeks "the Contraband Relief Association" was organized, with forty working members.

In September of 1862, Mrs. Lincoln left Washington for New York, and requested me to follow her in a few days, and join her at the Metropolitan Hotel. I was glad of the opportunity to do so, for I thought that in New York I would be able to do something in the interests of our society. Armed with credentials, I took the train for New York, and went to the Metropolitan, where Mrs. Lincoln had secured accommodations for me. The next morning I told Mrs. Lincoln of my project; and she immediately headed my list with a subscription of $200. I circulated among the colored people, and got them thoroughly interested in the subject, when I was called to Boston by Mrs. Lincoln, who wished to visit her son Robert, attending college in that city. I met Mr. Wendell Phillips, and other Boston philanthropists, who gave me all the assistance in their power. We held a mass meeting at the Colored Baptist Church, Rev. Mr. Grimes, in Boston, raised a sum of money, and organized there a branch society. The society was organized by Mrs. Grimes, wife of the pastor, assisted by Mrs. Martin, wife of Rev. Stella Martin. This branch of the main society, during the war, was able to send us over eighty large boxes of goods, contributed exclusively by the colored people of Boston. Returning to New York, we held a successful meeting at the Shiloh Church, Rev. Henry Highland Garnet, pastor. The Metropolitan Hotel, at that time as now, employed colored help. I suggested the object of my mission to Robert Thompson, steward of the hotel, who immediately raised quite a sum of money among the dining-room waiters. Mr. Frederick Douglass contributed $200, besides lecturing for us. Other prominent colored men sent in liberal contributions. From England a large quantity of stores was received. Mrs. Lincoln made frequent contributions, as also did the president. In 1863 I was reelected president of the association, which office I continue to hold.

For two years after Willie's death the White House was the scene of no fashionable display. The memory of the dead boy was duly respected. In some things Mrs. Lincoln was an altered woman. Sometimes, when in her room, with no one present but myself, the mere mention of Willie's name would excite her emotion, and any trifling memento that recalled him would move her to tears. She could not bear to look upon his picture; and after his death she never crossed the threshold of the Guest's Room in which he died, or the Green Room in which he was embalmed. There was something supernatural in her dread of these things, and something that she could not explain. Tad's nature was the opposite of Willie's, and he was always regarded as his father's favorite child. His black eyes fairly sparkled with mischief.

The war progressed, fair fields had been stained with blood, thousands of brave men had fallen, and thousands of eyes were weeping for the fallen at home. There were desolate hearthstones in the South as well as in the North, and as the people of my race watched the sanguinary struggle, the ebb and flow of the tide of battle, they lifted their faces Zionward, as if they hoped to catch a glimpse of the Promised Land beyond the sulphureous clouds of smoke which shifted now and then but to reveal ghastly rows of new-made graves. Sometimes the very life of the nation seemed to tremble with the fierce shock of arms. In 1863 the Confederates were flushed with victory, and sometimes it looked as if the proud flag of the Union, the glorious old Stars and Stripes, must yield half its nationality to the tri-barred flag that floated grandly over long columns of gray. These were sad, anxious days to Mr. Lincoln, and those who saw the man in privacy only could tell how much he suffered. One day he came into the room where I was fitting a dress on Mrs. Lincoln. His step was slow and heavy, and his face sad. Like a tired child he threw himself upon a sofa, and shaded his eyes with his hands. He was a complete picture of dejection. Mrs. Lincoln, observing his troubled look, asked: "Where have you been, Father?"

"To the War Department," was the brief, almost sullen answer.

"Any news?"

"Yes, plenty of news, but no good news. It is dark, dark everywhere."

He reached forth one of his long arms, and took a small Bible from a stand near the head of the sofa, opened the pages of the holy book, and soon was absorbed in reading them. A quarter of an hour passed, and on glancing at the sofa the face of the president seemed more cheerful. The dejected look was gone, and the countenance was lighted up with new resolution and hope. The change was so marked that I could not but wonder at it, and wonder led to the desire to know what book of the Bible afforded so much comfort to the reader. Making the search for a missing article an excuse, I walked gently around the sofa, and looking into the open book, I discovered that Mr. Lincoln was reading that divine comforter, Job. He read with Christian eagerness, and the courage and hope that he derived from the inspired pages made him a new man. I almost imagined that I could hear the Lord speaking to him from out the whirlwind of battle: "Gird up thy loins now like a man: I will demand of thee, and declare thou unto me."

What a sublime picture was this! A ruler of a mighty nation going to the pages of the Bible with simple Christian earnestness for comfort and courage, and finding both in the darkest hours of a nation's calamity. Ponder it, O ye scoffers at God's Holy Word, and then hang your heads for very shame!

Frequent letters were received warning Mr. Lincoln of assassination, but he never gave a second thought to the mysterious warnings. The letters, however, sorely troubled his wife. She seemed to read impending danger in every rustling leaf, in every whisper of the wind.

"Where are you going now, Father?" she would say to him, as she observed him putting on his overshoes and shawl.

"I am going over to the War Department, Mother, to try and learn some news."

"But, Father, you should not go out alone. You know you are surrounded with danger."

"All imagination. What does anyone want to harm me for? Don't worry about me, Mother, as if I were a little child, for no one is going to molest me."

And with a confident, unsuspecting air he would close the door behind him, descend the stairs, and pass out to his lonely walk.

For weeks, when trouble was anticipated, friends of the president would sleep in the White House to guard him from danger. Robert would come home every few months, bringing new joy to the family circle. He was very anxious to quit school and enter the army, but the move was sternly opposed by his mother.

"We have lost one son, and his loss is as much as I can bear, without being called upon to make another sacrifice," she would say, when the subject was under discussion.

"But many a poor mother has given up all her sons," mildly suggested Mr. Lincoln, "and our son is not more dear to us than the sons of other people are to their mothers."

"That may be; but I cannot bear to have Robert exposed to danger. His services are not required in the field, and the sacrifice would be a needless one."

"The services of every man who loves his country are required in this war. You should take a liberal instead of a selfish view of the question, Mother."

Argument at last prevailed, and permission was granted Robert to enter the army. With the rank of Captain and A.D.C. he went to the field, and remained in the army till the close of the war.

I well recollect a little incident that gave me a clearer insight into Robert's character. He was at home at the time the Tom Thumb combination was at Washington. The marriage of little Hopo'-my-thumb—Charles Stratton—to Miss Warren created no little excitement in the world, and the people of Washington participated in the general curiosity. Some of Mrs. Lincoln's friends made her believe that it was the duty of Mrs. Lincoln to show some attention to the remarkable dwarfs. Tom Thumb had been caressed by royalty in the Old World, and why should not the wife of the president of his native country smile upon him also? Verily, duty is one of the greatest bugbears in life. A hasty reception was arranged, and cards of invitation issued. I had dressed Mrs. Lincoln, and she was ready to go below and receive her guests, when Robert entered his mother's room.

"You are at leisure this afternoon, are you not, Robert?"

"Yes, Mother."

"Of course, then, you will dress and come downstairs."

"No, Mother, I do not propose to assist in entertaining Tom Thumb. My notions of duty, perhaps, are somewhat different from yours."

Robert had a lofty soul, and he could not stoop to all of the follies and absurdities of the ephemeral current of fashionable life.

Mrs. Lincoln's love for her husband sometimes prompted her to act very strangely. She was extremely jealous of him, and if a lady desired to court her displeasure, she could select no surer way to do it than to pay marked attention to the president. These little jealous freaks often were a source of perplexity to Mr. Lincoln. If it was a reception for which they were dressing, he would come into her room to conduct her downstairs, and while pulling on his gloves ask, with a merry twinkle in his eyes: "Well, Mother, who must I talk with tonight—shall it be Mrs. D.?"

"That deceitful woman! No, you shall not listen to her flattery."

"Well, then, what do you say to Miss C.? She is too young and handsome to practice deceit."

"Young and handsome, you call her! You should not judge beauty for me. No, she is in league with Mrs. D., and you shall not talk with her."

"Well, Mother, I must talk with someone. Is there anyone that you do not object to?" trying to button his glove, with a mock expression of gravity.

"I don't know as it is necessary that you should talk to anybody in particular. You know well enough, Mr. Lincoln, that I do not approve of your flirtations with silly women, just as if you were a beardless boy, fresh from school."

"But, Mother, I insist that I must talk with somebody. I can't stand around like a simpleton, and say nothing. If you will not tell me who I may talk with, please tell me who I may not talk with."

"There is Mrs. D. and Miss C. in particular. I detest them both. Mrs. B. also will come around you, but you need not listen to her flattery. These are the ones in particular."

"Very well, Mother; now that we have settled the question to your satisfaction, we will go downstairs;" and always with stately dignity, he proffered his arm and led the way.

Compiled by Huntington Theatre Company staff as accompanying material for its production of A Civil War Christmas. Behind the Scenes: Formerly a Slave, but More Recently Modiste, and Friend to Mrs. Abraham Lincoln, Or, Thirty Years a Slave, and Four Years in the White House, *by Elizabeth Keckley, was first published in 1868 by G. W. Carleton, publisher, New York.*

Specimen Days:

----◆----

Excerpts from Walt Whitman's Journal

A New York Soldier.

*T*his afternoon, July 22d, I have spent a long time with Oscar F. Wilber, Company G, 154th New York, low with chronic diarrhoea, and a bad wound also. He asked me to read him a chapter in the New Testament. I complied, and ask'd him what I should read. He said, "Make your own choice." I open'd at the close of one of the first books of the evangelists, and read the chapters describing the latter hours of Christ, and the scenes at the crucifixion. The poor, wasted young man ask'd me to read the following chapter also, how Christ rose again. I read very slowly, for Oscar was feeble. It pleased him very much, yet the tears were in his eyes. He ask'd me if I enjoy'd religion. I said, "Perhaps not, my dear, in the way you mean, and yet, may-be, it is the same thing." He said, "It is my chief reliance." He talk'd of death, and said he did not fear it. I said, "Why, Oscar, don't you think you will get well?" He said, "I may, but it is not probable." He spoke calmly of his condition. The wound was very bad, it discharg'd much. Then the diarrhoea had prostrated him, and

173

I felt that he was even then the same as dying. He behaved very manly and affectionate. The kiss I gave him as I was about leaving he return'd fourfold. He gave me his mother's address, Mrs. Sally D. Wilber, Alleghany post-office, Cattaraugus county, N.Y. I had several such interviews with him. He died a few days after the one just described.

HOME-MADE MUSIC.

August 8th.—To-night, as I was trying to keep cool, sitting by a wounded soldier in Armory-square, I was attracted by some pleasant singing in an adjoining ward. As my soldier was asleep, I left him, and entering the ward where the music was, I walk'd half-way down and took a seat by the cot of a young Brooklyn friend, S. R., badly wounded in the hand at Chancellorsville, and who has suffer'd much, but at that moment in the evening was wide awake and comparatively easy. He had turn'd over on his left side to get a better view of the singers, but the mosquito-curtains of the adjoining cots obstructed the sight. I stept round and loop'd them all up, so that he had a clear show, and then sat down again by him, and look'd and listen'd. The principal singer was a young lady-nurse of one of the wards, accompanying on a melodeon, and join'd by the lady-nurses of other wards. They sat there, making a charming group, with their handsome, healthy faces, and standing up a little behind them were some ten or fifteen of the convalescent soldiers, young men, nurses, &c., with books in their hands, singing. Of course it was not such a performance as the great soloists at the New York opera house take a hand in, yet I am not sure but I receiv'd as much pleasure under the circumstances, sitting there, as I have had from the best Italian compositions, express'd by world-famous performers. The men lying up and down the hospital, in their cots, (some badly wounded—some never to rise thence,) the cots themselves, with their drapery of white curtains, and the

174

shadows down the lower and upper parts of the ward; then the silence of the men, and the attitudes they took—the whole was a sight to look around upon again and again. And there sweetly rose those voices up to the high, whitewash'd wooden roof, and pleasantly the roof sent it all back again. They sang very well, mostly quaint old songs and declamatory hymns, to fitting tunes. Here, for instance:

> My days are swiftly gliding by, and I a pilgrim stranger,
> Would not detain them as they fly, those hours of toil
>   and danger;
> For O we stand on Jordan's strand, our friends are
>   passing over,
> And just before, the shining shore we may almost
>   discover.
> We'll gird our loins my brethren dear, our distant
>   home discerning,
> Our absent Lord has left us word, let every lamp be
>   burning,
> For O we stand on Jordan's strand, our friends are
>   passing over,
> And just before, the shining shore we may almost
>   discover.

ABRAHAM LINCOLN.

August 12th.—I see the President almost every day, as I happen to live where he passes to or from his lodgings out of town. He never sleeps at the White House during the hot season, but has quarters at a healthy location some three miles north of the city, the Soldiers' home, a United States military establishment. I saw him this morning about 8 1/2 coming in to business, riding on Vermont avenue, near L street. He always has a company of twenty-five or thirty cavalry, with sabres drawn and held upright over their shoulders. They say this guard was against his personal wish, but he let his counselors have their way. The party makes no great show in uniform or horses. Mr. Lincoln on the saddle generally rides a good-sized, easy-going gray horse, is dress'd in plain black, somewhat rusty and dusty, wears a black stiff hat, and looks about as ordinary in attire, &c., as the commonest man. A lieutenant, with yellow straps, rides at his left, and following behind, two by two, come the cavalry men, in their yellow-striped jackets. They are generally going at a slow trot, as that is the pace set them by the one they wait upon. The sabres and accoutrements clank, and the entirely unornamental *cortège* as it trots towards Lafayette square arouses no sensation, only some curious stranger stops and gazes. I see very plainly ABRAHAM LINCOLN's dark brown face, with the deep-cut lines, the eyes, always to me with a deep latent sadness in the expression. We have got so that we exchange bows, and very cordial ones. Sometimes the President goes and comes in an open barouche. The cavalry always accompany him, with drawn sabres. Often I notice as he goes out evenings—and sometimes in the morning, when he returns early—he turns off and halts at the large and handsome residence of the Secretary of War, on K street, and holds conference there. If in his barouche, I can see from my window he does not alight, but sits in his vehicle, and Mr. Stanton comes out to attend him. Sometimes one of his sons, a boy of ten or twelve, accompanies him, riding at his right on a pony. Earlier in the summer I occasionally saw the President and his wife, towards the latter part of the afternoon, out in a barouche, on a pleasure ride through the city. Mrs. Lincoln was dress'd in complete black, with a long crape veil. The equipage is of the plainest kind, only two horses, and they nothing extra. They pass'd me once very close, and I saw the President in the face fully, as they were moving slowly, and his look, though abstracted, happen'd to be directed steadily in my eye. He bow'd and smiled, but far beneath his smile I noticed well the expression I have alluded to. None of the artists or pictures has caught the deep, though subtle and indirect expression of this man's face. There is something else there. One of the great portrait painters of two or three centuries ago is needed.

Soldiers and Talks.

Soldiers, soldiers, soldiers, you meet everywhere about the city, often superb-looking men, though invalids dress'd in worn uniforms, and carrying canes or crutches. I often have talks with them, occasionally quite long and interesting. One, for instance, will have been all through the peninsula under McClellan— narrates to me the fights, the marches, the strange, quick changes of that eventful campaign, and gives glimpses of many things untold in any official reports or books or journals. These, indeed, are the things that are genuine and precious. The man was there, has been out two years, has been through a dozen fights, the superfluous flesh of talking is long work'd off him, and he gives me little but the hard meat and sinew. I find it refreshing, these hardy, bright, intuitive, American young men (experienc'd soldiers with all their youth). The vocal play and significance moves one more than books. Then there hangs something majestic about a man who has borne his part in battles, especially if he is very quiet regarding it when you desire him to unbosom. I am continually lost at the absence of blowing and blowers among these old-young American militaires. I have found some man or other who has been in every battle since the war began, and have talk'd with them about each one in every part of the United States, and many of the engagements on the rivers and harbors too. I find men here from every State in the Union, without exception. (There are more Southerners, especially border State men, in the Union army than is generally supposed.) I now doubt whether one can get a fair idea of what this war practically is, or what genuine America is, and her character, without some such experience as this I am having.

A SILENT NIGHT RAMBLE.

October 20th.—To-night, after leaving the hospital at 10 o'clock, (I had been on self-imposed duty some five hours, pretty closely confined,) I wander'd a long time around Washington. The night was sweet, very clear, sufficiently cool, a voluptuous half-moon, slightly golden, the space near it of a transparent blue-gray tinge. I walk'd up Pennsylvania avenue, and then to Seventh street, and a long while around the Patent-office. Somehow it look'd rebukefully strong, majestic, there in the delicate moonlight. The sky, the planets, the constellations all so bright, so calm, so expressively silent, so soothing, after those hospital scenes. I wander'd to and fro till the moist moon set, long after midnight.

Compiled by Huntington Theatre Company staff, as accompanying material to its production of A Civil War Christmas. Specimen Days, *by Walt Whitman, was first published in 1882 by David McKay, publisher, Philadelphia.*